The Idea of South Sudan

The History of Political Thought

John Gai Yoh

Africa
World Books
Pty Ltd

Table of Contents

CHAPTER TWO

The Development of the Southern Sudanese
Political Groups, 1948 – 1957

CHAPTER THREE

The Emergence of Southern Sudanese Political Parties:
1958-70

CHAPTER FOUR
Southern Sudan Organizations Inside the Sudan 161

Dedication

Phelimon Majok,

Clement Mboro,

James Tembura,

Both Diu,

Chief Lolik Lado,

Siricio Iro,

Edward Adhok,

Lueth Ajak,

Kunyangi Ababa,

Hassan Fertak,

Chief Cir Rehan,

Chief Gir Kiro,

Pastor Andrea Apaya,

Chief Ukuma Bazia,

Chief Lappanya,

Father Guido Akou,

Chief Tet

Acknowledgements

The Idea of South Sudan was the original topic I decided to research on for my Masters degree program, before I was persuaded to shift to another topic. The original question I had in mind, was how did South Sudan become an entity within Sudan and where did the idea originated from? Who were the architects of the concept of Southern Sudan? How did the Turks, British, Belgians, Portuguese, French and the Egyptians become part of Southern Sudan political history? Who were the South Sudanese pioneers in politics of Sudan? How did the political and social organizations develop in Southern Sudan? How did Southern Sudan become a political community?

All these questions prompted me to read different literature on the colonial history of Sudan and Egypt and eventually wrote this book as an attempt to provide answers to these questions.

This research was carried out at different stages, culminating in its current shape in 2002, covering the period between 1890s and 1972.

Eng. Farouk Gatkuoth Kam and several friends who read the Arabic translation of the book has encouraged me to publish the English version so as to give access to those who cannot read Arabic.

I am grateful to Dr. Douglas H. Johnson who encouraged me and introduced me to Africa World Books publisher, Peter Deng who kindly published the book.

Introduction

~

The great migrations of Africans which took place in big waves in the turn of 3rd century A.D. have had great impact in shaping what became the Sudan and subsequently shaped the characteristics of the people who inhabited it since then in terms of evolution of its civilizations, cultures, philosophical ideas to the extent that the whole of what is today western, central and eastern Africa could be described as nations in transition.

The people of Sudan, which accounts for over 500 ethnic groups, are therefore by products of this great migration. The penetration of this region by other civilizations such as the Roman and Byzantine Empires all of which culminated into Christian and Islamic civilizations manifested themselves in terms of the Ottoman Empire and the European imperial expansion.

The history of the people of Sudan has been influenced by these external interventions some of which continued not only in the Sudan but the rest of Africa at least from the 17th

Century onwards. The Sudan, from historical perspective, was influenced through four routes of migration.

The North African route has influenced the migration of the Nilotic people into the interior of Sudan and the highlands of Ethiopia, while the Western and Central African migration pushed the inhabitants of what today is Darfur and Kordufan to where they are today. The Eastern and Southern migration route settled in what is today Ethiopia and East Africa which included Kenya, Tanzania and Uganda.

The political, economic and social history of South Sudan or the idea of South Sudan should therefore be studied within this wider context. The most influential cultural and political influences that shaped the geopolitical history of South Sudan are the Turkish rule and European imperial system characterized by West Minister system of governance and Christianity while the Arab and Islamic culture has had great impact on the rest of Sudan, which through association extended to South Sudan.

The idea of South Sudan was therefore a creation of all the factors mentioned above, although the Turks, British and the Egyptians influence could be credited for concretizing the geographical location of what is today the Republic of South Sudan.

The "problem of Southern Sudan" was never confined to South Sudan as historians tried to argue, rather it was part of Islamic and European civilizations attempt to reshape Africa to achieve their "civilizational project". In 1884 this goal was achieved when Africa was divided into spheres of influence in which Sudan and Egypt became Great Britain protectorates and slowly the influence of the Ottomans declined, subsequently paving the way for the Great Britain and Egypt to sign the famous Anglo-Egyptian Condominium Agreement on Sudan in 1899.

This book therefore attempts to reflect on the political ideas that shaped what is today South Sudan. This study traces the history of political thought in South Sudan through 5 phases:

First, the people of Sudan and in particular the people of South Sudan came into contacts with external civilizations as represented by the Ottomans, Egyptians, Great Britain, French, Portuguese and Italians all of whom tried in different ways to pacify or force the people of South Sudan to succumb to their rules and in the process left behind traces of their governance systems and cultures.

Secondly, the expansion of Islam and Arab cultures in what was then Northern Sudan, culminated into complete takeover of the Sudan by the Mahadia regime during the period between 1884-1898 and introduced the Arabic and Islamic culture in Sudan as a result of which South Sudan became victim of forced Islamization and slavery.

Thirdly, the Condominium Agreement between Great Britain and Egypt in 1899 resulting in declaration of Sudan as protectorate of the two countries and the Great Britain has become the defacto ruler of Sudan, hence introducing indirect rule system, which divided Sudan administratively into ethnic enclaves.

Fourthly, the decision by the Great Britain to give Sudan

Self-rule in 1953 meant that the administrative and political powers of Great Britain and Egypt were transferred to North Sudanese sectarian elites who used Arabism and political Islam as tools for extending their domination to South Sudan. The reaction of the people of South Sudan towards the new rulers in Khartoum was confrontational.

Finally, the politics of independence in Sudan created tensions between North Sudanese political elites who ideologically depicted themselves as Arab Muslims group while the South Sudanese and later on the other African communities in Sudan presented themselves as African and in case of the South a Christian group.

The conflict over the identity of Sudan therefore produced two contradictory ideological visions for what Sudan represented. The development of political organizations in South Sudan during the period 1920s-1972 is the history that this book attempts to relate. It is a history of political ideas that were later on transformed into political and military organizations, each on its own ways tried to achieve what was the core of conflict that is political and socio-economic identity for the people of South Sudan.

CHAPTER 1

Southern Sudan Policy, 1899-1947

~

After the overthrow of the Mahdist state in 1898, the question of the future status of the Sudan soon posed itself. To find a lasting solution to this problem, Lord Cromer, the British Consul-General in Egypt, devised what he called 'a suitable' solution to the problem of the Sudan's status. With neither annexation by British nor incorporation under the Khadivate, he suggested a 'hybrid' form of government, which honored Egyptian claims and safeguarded British interests. This 'solution' was in 1899, best known to historians as 'Anglo-Egyptian-Condominium Agreement'. This Agreement created theoretically joint Anglo-Egyptian sovereignty over the Sudan. British claims were based on the 'right of conquest', while those of Egypt were defined by reference to 'certain provinces in the Sudan which were in rebellion against the authority of his Highness the Khadive'.

Based on this Agreement Sudan became Anglo-Egyptian protectorate, co-governed by the two governments.

Unlike in Southern Sudan, the new Anglo-Egyptian rulers did not encounter important resistance in Northern Sudan. This could be attributed to a) the Northern Sudanese, with exception of few Mahdist loyalists, did not detect, instantly, any threat posed by the new rulers. In fact, most of those who inhibited the Eastern and Northern most of the country were in one way or another anti-Mahdists. Instead, it was in the Western and central regions that pro-Mahdists hopelessly tried to create problems to the British. b) The educated elites and civil servants, most of whom were pro-Egypt, chose to coop- erate with the new government and c) while northern Sudan was accessible to the new government both by sea and land, the new rulers did not find difficulty in understanding cultural and political identity of the northern Sudanese. This was because the Egyptians, being partners to the Condominium, had long presence in Northern Sudan, which allowed them to know Northern Sudanese political and religious affiliation.[1]

However, the situation in the Southern Sudan was completely different. Southern Sudanese social, geograph- ical and political attitudes varied compared to those in the north. The Shilluk tribe was relatively, like Anuak tribe, unified under their divine king or *reth*. The Azande were organized in militant principalities in Western Equatoria were engaged in their local tribal conflicts. The Nuer in Upper Nile, have loose political organization, and to them the village was the largest unit of the society. The Dinka's authority was wielded by heredity or cult figures depended on personal prestige.[2]

In other words, the Southern Sudan was virtually unknown to those who were called upon to rule it; and as we shall see, sometimes it was risky to go there. The government was faced by three main problems in the South; inaccessibility of the region; shortages of the staff and funds, and the fierce resistance that the Southern Sudanese tribes posed against the new intruders.

Pacification and Resistance in the South

The main task to be done in the south by the new government in 1898 was to extend and secure its river communication as a first step. The work at hand was to carry out road-clearance and maintenance, the construction and repair of guesthouses along the main roads throughout the South; and a monopoly of ivory or any other mineral resources available in the South. Ironically though, the ultimate humanitarian aim of the new rulers was to 'teach these savages the elements of common sense, good behavior and obedience to the government authority'.[3]

The first government mission to the South was led by Major Malcolm Peake, who was supposed to head to Bahr al-Jabal and Bahr al-Ghazal in October 1898. On his way he was confronted by the *Sudd*, best known as 'Grass curtain', and could not move more than about (180 miles). Reporting back to H.W. Jackson the then administrator at Fashoda (currently Kodok) Peake had this to say:

*"When the steamer could not traced no further
owing to shallow water and the Sudd, I went on ½
a mile in Faluka (small boat) and having climbed a
tree, I could see nothing beyond or around but reeds
and patches of water at intervals."*[4]

Based on the above report, the Sudan government decided to do something about the Grass Curtain. In 1901 the government approved a Sudd-clearing expedition. It took the government four expeditions before the main channel of Bahr al-Jabal was finally cleared on the winter of 1904-5. The same task was carried out in Bahr al-Ghazal in 1900-1 and 1902. In the meantime, the entire government of Southern Sudan was based in Fashoda until 1901 when Bahr al-Ghazal was consti-tuted as a province with its headquarters at Wau. In 1903 the Fashoda Administration became first class province, Upper Nile Province. In January 1st, 1906 Mongalla Province was established to include the Southern part of the Upper Nile Province. Between 1900-1906, Wau, Tonj, Shambe, Rumbek, and Duyem al-Zubayer in Bahr al-Ghazal were occupied by the British.[5]

To the South of Wau lay prince-doms of Azande tribe. By the time the British arrived the Azande had already experience of Europeans, through Turco-Egyptian rulers, private traders, the French and the Belgians. The interference of these powers made the situation more complex in which the various Azande communities fought each other. The first Azande king with whom the British came into contact was Tembura. Tembura's

Kingdom was inhabited mainly by non-Azande subjects. To the South he competed with other Azande rulers, notably Yambio.

In the event of hostilities with the rival, Tembura realized the necessity of cooperation with British; on that effect he sent envoys to Bahr al-Ghazal Governor, offering gifts and peace. On the other hand, Yambio attempted to match Tembura influence by sending his grandson to Wau with valuable gifts of ivory. In January 1904 the Yambio Battalion consisting two hundred men of the 15th Sudanese Batalion, under command of Major Wood set out. This expedition resulted in a violent confrontation at the village of Riketa, with another of Yambio's sons, in which the Azande lost six dead and the patrol two. Meanwhile, promises of cooperation and assistance had been received from Tembura.

Realizing that his power was broken, Yambio sent a word to the Belgians declaring his submission in hope that this would foretell the British invasion, but it was too late. The government advanced, Yambio refused to surrender and was eventually mortally wounded during an attempt at flight.[6] The resistance that followed was insignificant and most of the Azande princes submitted without struggle. With the collapse of the Azande resistance the Sudan government established the foundations of administration in Western Equatoria, and three districts, Maridi, Tambura, and Yambio were established.

In the Bahr al-Ghazal region the confrontation between the Anglo-Egyptian government and the Dinka tribe took three stages:

In January 1902 the Agar Dinka led by chief Manyang Mathiang, rose in rebellion after the British governor in the region ordered them to return cattle taken during a raid on another Dinka section. The Agar reacted violently and ambushed a government column killing its commander, captain Scott-Barbour, and few others. The government retaliated by launching two expeditions, first by Captain W.H. Hunter, then by major Lee Stack. The Agar country was wrecked to the "point that not more than a dozen houses were left standing in the district of Rumbek".[7] The Agar suppression was meant partly as a 'warning to the rest of the Dinka sections';[8] but it seemed the message, if not misunderstood, was completely ignored by the other Dinka sections.

The second rebellion of Dinka' was by the Atwot Dinka section in 1909, 1913 and 1917 consecutively. Many expeditions were sent to the region and both sides lost considerably. It was not until May 1918 that the Atwot rebellion was pacified.[9]

Still in the Bahr al-Ghazal region, another Dinka revolt arose in October 1919. This time by the Aliab section. Upon the news was received of a possible Aliab uprising, a column under Major R. White was sent to abort the expected rebellion. While on its way, the column was ambushed on 16 November 1919 with loss of seven men. On December 2nd, White, the Commandant of Equatorial Battalion, was reinforced by Major C.H. Stignand, himself the Governor of Mongalla Province. On the 8th December their column was attacked by about a thousand Aliab youth, both Stignand and White were killed, as well as an Egyptian officer and twenty-two soldiers. The Aliab rebellion was eventually suppressed in 1920.[10]

In the final analysis it is possible to say that in both cases in Bhar al-Ghazal and in Azande land, the revolts were caused either by the what was perceived by the local population as government's policy of 'giving nothing but taking taxes and labour' i.e. the government's reliance solely on the use of force of arms, or the traditional fear of the inhabitants of these regions towards foreign rulers.

Whatever were the causes underlying the Dinka and the Azande land revolts, the situation in the upper Nile Province was even more complicated for the new government to handle.

Among the upper Nile tribes, the Shillluk and other Dinka minor sections did not pose any significant resistance to the new rules. This could be attributed to the following:

The geographical locality of the Shilluk area at the northern most of the province gave the Shilluk a special political situation. Throughout their political history the Shilluk were often the first to be encountered by any foreign power that entered Southern Sudan. In the long ran this led to conclusion of peaceful agreements between Shilluk and central governments in the North. The agreements, often invalidated by the lack of trust, created some sort of political awareness and understanding between the Shilluk divine kings (reths) and various Khartoum governments.

The new Sudan government chose to cooperate with the Shilluk King (reth), whose authority among Shilluk is unchallenged. By doing so the British were able to cooperate with Shilluk through their divine king. [11]

It was, however, in the Nuerland that the British encountered furious resistance in the Upper Nile province. The Nuer resistance grew mainly out of the tradition of inter-tribal warfare predating the coming of the British government. In principle, in the Nuer perception, the British were not different from the Turco-Egyptians (Turuk), Europeans (missionaries), and the Mahdists who had preceded them up the Nile; "non of these governments had been able to administered the Nuer in even the loosest sense".[12] However, the new government's policy of favouring the neighbouring Dinka in their relations with the Nuer discounted, unconsciously perhaps, a long tradition of Nuer-Dinka cooperation, a fact, which a British officer could not comprehend.

The Sudan government's first contact with the Nuer was in 1899, at the time that it was the new government's policy to win the submission of all the Southern tribal chiefs. The government, unaware of the Nuer's customs and traditions, failed to know that these chiefs in Nuer's understanding meant Nguondeng Bong and Dual Diu. These were not chiefs, rather they were, in political sense, symbols of the tribe "who possessed the spirit of the sky God".[13] They were feared, respected and influential among their people, but had no political authority.

In September 1901 a Nuer raid on their neighbour, the Anuak tribe, was reported. The government reacted by invading the Nuerland in April 1902, under Blewitt Ben, whose

21

mission was to receive the submission of Nguondeng, sometimes referred to as 'Deng Kur'. Another patrol was launched in 1905 under Major Wilson into the Nuerland; villages were burned and cattle were confiscated. As a result, raids on the Bor Dinka villages by the Nuer increased, partly because the Nuer wanted to show their defiance to the British invaders or presumably they wanted to compensate their confiscated cattle. Two years later Nguondeng and Diu died, 1906 and 1907 consecutively.[14]

With intensification of the violence between the Nuer and the Bor Dinka a boundary has to be demarcated between the two tribes.[15] This boundary was to correspond to the boundary between Upper Nile and Mongalla provinces.

Meanwhile, the Anuak's acquisition of firearms from Ethiopia pressurized the Eastern Nuers to demand the government protection. In respond to their demand, the government launched an attack in March 1912, commanded by Major C.H. Levenson, into Anuak territory; in the battle the government lost 50 killed including two British officers.

It has to be noted that the Nuer in general had always seen their payment of taxes as payment for government protection. In the same manner, the Bor Dinka in return to their cooperation demanded the government protection. The Nuer argued that if the government could not or would not protect them there was no reason for them to pay taxes, let alone cooperation, which implied submission. This last point was consolidated when in 1914 the government distributed firearms to the Bor Dinka for self-defense.[16] Most importantly, by imposing the Nuer-Dinka boundary the government, unintentionally perhaps, introduced into the Nuer-Dinka the rivalry of its own officials. In other words, by creating boundary and distributing firearms to Dinka, the Nuer looked upon the Mongalla province authorities as allies of the Bor Dinka.

Still in Upper Nile Province, it has to be recalled that the relations between the Bor Dinka and the Murle tribe were often characterized by continuous conflict. The Murle, inhabiting the Pibor valley, had a history of raiding the Bor section of Dinka. In 1908 a patrol was sent against the Murle, many cattle were taken, however, the mission failed to achieve Murle submission, the main objective of the Mission. In January 1912 another expedition was launched; four months later the Murle, after a heavy lost, announced their tactical submission.[17]

In general, it was not till late 1920s that most of the Upper Nile tribes were pacified. The last tribe to be pacified was the Nuer. In January 1929, the foreign office in London, along with Anglo-Egyptian authorities in Khartoum and Cairo, finally approved the 'policy of Nuer settlement'. It was also decided that the policy of 'no-man-land' between Nuer and Dinka be strengthened. On February 8th, 1929, during an attack by the Province police, Guek Nguondeng, son of Dengkur, was killed.[18] Further land and air operations were undertaken in March in Lou land. With 'Nuer settlemont' the Sudan government began to think seriously of a proper policy through which it can administer Southern Sudan.

In the South-East of the Equatoria the government's administration came rather late. The Didinga tribe was brought under government control after their continuous raids across Uganda border alerted the government and hence necessitated its intervention. In February 1922 a post was established at Nagicot. The Sudan government's troops were not removed in this post until the Uganda officials had founded the basis for future administration in January 1923.[19] A similar problem was posed by the Toposa, whose land marched with Kenya and Ethiopia. Several times the government tried to establish posts in their territories, but all efforts went in vain. In 1924, at Kitgum, representatives of the Anglo-Egyptian government and their counterparts in Uganda and Kenya met to discuss a solution by which the so-called "Ilemi Triangle" would be ceded to Kenya and Toposa land occupied by the Sudan government.[20] Although this arrangement was accepted by the three parties; the Toposa raids on the Kenya administered Turkana tribe continued. It was not until 1924 that the government finally resolved to occupy Toposa land: and this decision was implemented by the Equatorial Battalion in December 1926. As a result, a post was established at Kapoeta in May 1927.

It seems plausible therefore to say that the first three decades of British presence in the Southern Sudan were devoted mainly to the achievement of two objectives:

First, pacification of southern tribes, and second establishment of administrative units or districts in various pacified parts of the South.[21] This difficult task, though achieved at last, necessitated military intervention, without which it would have taken Anthropologists longer time to achieve.

Yet, during this period the British administrators acknowledged that differences and conditions in the South and those in Northern Sudan were 'unbridgeable gap'. In their opinion, "the South was an area of speculation no more comprehensible than the human mind, mysterious, unknown and better be left that way."[22]

They further thought that the inclusion of this vast territory within the Sudan's borders was adventurous result of imperial politics that added no benefit to the country as a whole, but exhausted it of scant resources. In fact, the government was seen by the Southern tribes as "only the latest in a series of foreign intruders who raided and taxes, plundered and killed, promised security and did not provide it, came and went; instead of peace, with continuous unrest, instead of administration there were a series of posts designed to keep one tribe from another".[23]

The government for most these tribes was some sort of incomprehensible illusive entity located in some distance place in Khartoum or in London which, in their opinion, occasionally interfered in their lives with instructions brought in person of some official with few servants and policemen.[24]

In the final analysis, it could be inferred from what is discussed that Southern tribes did not coordinate their resistance against the British authority in the South. In fact, each tribe cared much for its own security more than the lost of incomprehensible 'entity' called 'Southern Sudan'. Therefore, among Southerners of those days, the concept of a 'Southern Sudan entity' did not exist in its political sense.

The Search for a Southern Policy

While the Anglo-Egyptian officers were preoccupied pacifying the Southern tribes, the central government in Khartoum was undertaking plans to establish 'Foundations' through which the pacified Southern region would be administered. Based on Mr. Viscount Milner Report in 1921, the government suggested that the South "was to be ruled through native authorities under government supervision".[25]

To that effect chief courts and traditional authorities were encouraged in those posts or districts, which the government troops controlled. In order to strengthen the government position in the South, the governors in the South recommended to the Governor-General the following steps to be taken:

The governors suggested the establishment of Southern Sudanese army; their argument was based on the fact that:

> "... as the army is a great mission agent and all the Sudanese _askari_ made a point of seeing that every recruit does become a Muslim and the imams instruct them Kur'an, an Equatorial Battalion be formed for service in the South composed entirely of Southerners and the commands of which would be in English and the observances of which would be Christian".[26]

The Governor-General, Wingate, approved the plan. His decision was based on his own knowledge of what he referred to as "Sudanese religious feeling". This feeling, he argued,

26

expressed itself in "numerous local outbursts against British in the South". The Equatorial corps, the only dominated Southern institution was established and on December 7th, 1917, the last of the northern Sudanese troops left Mongalla. The Equatorial Garrison became the only permanent military garrison in the Southern Sudan until its mutiny in August 1955.

In 1918, Sunday was recognized throughout the South as the official day of the rest. English was adopted as the official language of the South. Later on, at the Rejaf Language Conference in 1928, the government accepted recommendations to develop local languages. Bari, Shiluk, Nuer, Latuka, Dinka and Azande were chosen as "group languages" to be taught at elementary level.[27]

The above steps were necessitated by the following new realities of the time:

1. By the end of the First World War, the British Colonial attitude toward its subjects changed dramatically. In addition, victorious powers became aware of the moral obligations towards their subjects. Moreover, the creation of the League of Nations directed attention to the need to develop the socalled 'backward societies' in which Southern Sudan was not, but a small part.

2. The missionary societies in the colonial territories acquired, after the war, a new role and decided to cooperate with governments more actively in the field of education and health services.

3. The rise of the Northern Sudanese nationalism after the war, pioneered by the educated elite, and closely associated

with the Egyptian nationalists, caused much alarm to the Sudan government. As such, the Sudan's political status by 1915 was linked to what the British regarded as an Egyptian problem. It has often been Sudan government policy to discourage a future link between Egypt and Sudan; in the same manner, the British authorities were not prepared to link South's future with that of the Northern Sudan, hence with Egypt.

4. Through its emphasis on the "Indirect Rule" and the need to protect the "Pagan tribes of the South", (contrary to what was taking place on the ground) against foreign influences', mainly the Islamic influence, the Sudan government concluded that the "South must be ruled differently from the North".[28]

Again, the impact of the above developments urged and made it necessary for the government to devise some sort of 'policy', which must be calculated and carefully arranged to govern the South separately from the North, at least temporarily.

In a memorandum addressed to the Milner Mission, the Sudan government, for the first time, indicated that the government policy was to keep out Islamic influences from the Southern Sudan and suggested that:

> *"the possibility of Southern (Black) portion of the Sudan being eventually cut off from the Northern (Arab) area and linked up with some central African system should be borne in mind."*[29]

In another memorandum concerning the South, Mathew, the Secretary of Education and Health wrote to the Civil secretary that:

"in time we shall reap our own advantage, for a series of self-contained racial units will be developed – based on the solid rock of indigenous traditions and beliefs -- and in the process a solid barrier will be created against the indigenous intrigue which must in the ordinary course of events increasingly beset our path in the North".[30]

In another memorandum the government suggested that:

"... boundaries between the North and the South be drawn along a line from East to West following Baro river and Sobat river Nile, the White Nile and Bahr al-Ghazal rivers".31

In order to consolidate the above suggestions, the government initiated, between 1920 and 1930, the following steps in the South:

In 1921 the three governors of the South were permitted not to attend all the meeting of all nine governors held annually as the tradition required. The Governor-General advised them instead to have their own gatherings in the South and keep in touch with their counterparts in Kenya and Uganda. The Governor-General justified his decision by arguing that:

"... a natural division has emerged between those

provinces which are accessible and those are not, in that it has only been possible to collect the former in Khartoum – this decision has been found to correspond exactly between the Arab and the Negroid portions of the Sudan, for all the former provinces, Halfa, Dongola, Berber , Red Sea , Blue Nile , Sennar ,White Nile , Khartoum are converted with Khartoum by rail way , whereas the nearest of the Negroid provinces is approached only by river and is not less than five days away – the governors of the latter , therefore , meet separately at some convenient place on the river, South of Khartoum (Southern Sudan)".[32]

In 1922, the Passports and Permits Ordinance (1922) was promulgated. By this ordinance the Governor-General was empowered to declare any part of the Sudan a ' Closed District or Area'. The Governor-General was allowed by article (22) of the Ordinance to declare any district in the country as absolutely or partially closed for Sudanese or non-Sudanese; in the same Ordinance in article (23) he was given the right to close any part of the Sudan to external trade or " for trading other than the inhabitants of the area"[33] Article 28A (i) also empowered him to prohibit the engagement of Labour in any part of the Sudan for employment or outside the Sudan.

In the same year, " Closed District Order" (1922) was issued which declared the whole of the Darfur, Equatoria, Bahr al-Ghazal, Upper Nile, parts of the Northern Kordufan, Gizien, Kassalla provinces as 'Closed Districts'. The ordinance went on to explain that:

> *"the extend that no person other than a native of the Sudan shall enter or remain therein unless he is a holder of a permit in his behalf to be obtained from the Civil Secretary or from the Governor of the Province in which the Closed District is situated, and that any native of the Province in which the Closed District is situated, and that any native of the Sudan may be forbidden to enter or remain in the said Districts by Civil Secretary or Governor of such province."[34]*

In 1921, the government decided to support and encourage the missionary education in the South. The Governor-General stated that it was the government responsibility to regulate and supervise some of the missionary services, mainly education along new lines responsive to more immediate benefit to the government. This would be accomplished through grant-in-aid system; the grant would help in establishment of two years advance course in missionary schools for those students who had completed their education at these schools. It was hoped that the graduates of the new advance courses would replace the Northern administrators and clerks working in the South. As a result, a system of grant-in-aid was approved in 1927. Eventually the numbers of schools and students increased.[35]

(see Table 1).

Table 1

Number of Village Schools	1927	1932	1934	1936	1938
Number of Elementary Schools (Boys)	27	189	310	392	585
Number of Elementary Schools (Girls)	-	5	16	17	18
Number of Intermediate Schools (Boys)	3	3	3	3	3
Number of Trade Schools (Boys)	2	3	3	3	3
Number of Normal Schools (Boys)	-	1	2	3	2

The Fifth Ordinance was issued in 1925. The permits to the Trade Order (1925) stated that, no person other than native was allowed to carry on trade without a permit permitting him to trade in the South. The Order specified that no Northern Sudanese trade (normally called by Southerners as Jallaba) will be allowed to trade in the South, unless he is permitted by the Governor of the province concerned to do so.[36]

The permits to the Trade Order (1928) ordered that no native in the three Southern provinces "shall trade in any goods other than local produce which shall not be deemed to include ivory in any place outside the market of the District, unless he had been permitted to do so."[37]

The above policies, and many more others, ultimately

resulted in a progressive exclusion of northern officials and traders and by and large limited the Southerners travelling to the North. In fact, all these actions were directed towards consolidation of a future administrative control in the South. In other words, there was a need for a policy to be followed in the South.

However, we must be cautious in asserting that there was a tendency toward separating the South from the North. In fact, in these early years the tendency toward a 'separate policy for the South' was uncoordinated; instead it was based by and large on the government's fear of Islam as a threat to its own security. Moreover, the British officials in the South saw in the elimination of the Northern presence in the South as an end by itself, rather than a condition necessary for the development of the 'Indirect Rule' or as it was called the 'Native Administration' in the South.

The elimination of the Northern Sudanese received more attention than their replacement; thus in the South very little, if any, was done to train and promote Southerners who would replace the outgoing Northerners.[38] Furthermore, the few Southerners who acquired missionary education suffered the same disability in the eyes of these British officials. The half-educated Southerner was 'detribalized', had ideas of his own, could not be trusted and no place for him in his own traditional society. As the time passed the British administrators began to envy the half-educated Southerners, hence restricted them to perform clerical work, which they often avoid to do.[39]

The Southern Policy of 1930

The official formulation of what became known as 'Southern Policy' in 1930 was already in conflict with the pattern of the emerging administration in the South. These contradictions can be classified into three opposing extremes.

The administrative pattern that existed in the South in 1920's aimed at creation of a 'Southern Literate Class'. This pattern was in principle hostile to the policy of Indirect Rule where the Tribal Chiefs were to be the source of civil authority.

Few chiefs who were recognized by the government were not unacknowledged by the people over whom they were supposed to have traditional powers; thus, their powers were challenged by their own people.

The British administrators in the South were consistently hesitating to delegate a real power: and as they began to gain local experience and partially won the confident of the local people, they began to employ more 'direct methods'. Thus, the prestige of the tribal chiefs was entirely dependent on the District Commissioners.[40]

The 'Southern policy' was formulated in form of a memorandum, addressed to the three governors of the South, by Sir Harold Mac-Michael on January 25, 1930. He started by saying:

> "His Excellency the Governor-General directs that the main features of the approved policy of the government for the administration of the Southern provinces should be re-stated in simple terms."[41]

Mac Michael's memorandum reiterated what had already been taking place practically in the South. The basic principles raised by the memorandum were 'to build up a series of self-contained racial or tribal units with structure and organization' based on what he called traditional usage and beliefs; transfer of the northern administrators in the South and their replacement by the Southern Sudanese; the use of English where communication in the local vernacular was impossible, especially among the police and the Southern corps. It has to be noted that only (24) District Commissioners were fluent in local vernacularism in 1932.

The fourth principle was the control of emigrant traders from the North. The new policy aimed at encouragement of Greek labour and Syrian Christians, rather than *Jallaba* type to trade in the South. Permits to the later should be decreased, while permissions to the former were to increase.[42]

Furthermore, the Civil Secretary emphasized the following points to be put into consideration by the Southern governors:

That the execution of the proposed new policy may lead to financial commitments; thus the governors were advised to report back to the Governor-General who was in turn will be ready to provide any time the necessary assistance.

The implementation of the proposed policy was expected to vary from locality to another: it was therefore hoped that the ultimate objective will be to execute it no matter the difficulty that may be encountered from such a situation.

On the other hand, the 1930 Southern policy was seen

by the government as a well-planned program to be pursued progressively. Based on this program, the approved policy of the government was to:

> *"... act upon the fact that the peoples of the Southern Sudan are distinctly African and Negroid"*[43]

and that the Sudan government's obvious duty

> *"is to push ahead as fast as it can with their economic and educational development on African and Negroid lines and not upon the Middle Eastern and Arab Lines".*[44]

As to how the objectives of the new policy would be achieved, the memorandum went on to say that it is

> *"... only by economic and educational development that these people of the south can be equipped to stand up for themselves whether their lot can be eventually cast with the northern Sudan or with East Africa".*[45]

In other words, it was the government policy to encourage Southerners to resist, as a large and cohesive ethnic minority the attitude of the more sophisticated Arab north; and that should their lot be casted with East Africa, Southerners would have ability to catch up with them.

In order to implement the new policy many suggestions and counter suggestions were made concerning introduction of administrative reforms in Southern Sudan. It has to be noted that until 1936 there were three provinces in the South, Mongalla, Bahr al-Gazal and Upper Nile.

In 1937 a suggestion was forwarded to the Governor-General, and later approved, to merge Mongalla province into Bahr al-Ghazal and Eqhatoria both with one governor. The mergence of Mongalla was seen as a first step toward the incorporation of Upper Nile into a regional government of the South. Such measures were viewed by Northern intellectuals as ultimately aimed at separating the South from North. However, the government argued that if the educational and economic development in the South, which already took place in the North, was to be achieved, major changes in the provisional administration was necessary.

On the other hand, the advent of the Southern policy meant very little change in the administration and daily life in the South. In fact, to the Southern Sudanese the change was more in minds of the Northern Sudanese, who considered the policy as a giant step towards separating the South from the North; and if at all, the Southern policy have had significant impact on the British administrators than upon individual Southerners, because indeed, there was only limited 'Southern participation' in the decision making process in the country at that time.[46]

The Abrogation of the 1930 Southern Policy

The reaction of the Northern Graduate Congress towards the 1930 Southern policy, was submitted to the government in a memorandum in 1942 in which they demanded:

1. The abolition of the 'Closed Districts' Ordinances';
2. Lifting of the restrictions on trade and movements of the Sudanese within the Sudan;
3. The cancellation of the financial aid to the missionaries.
4. They also insisted that the educational syllabuses in the North and the South be unified.[47]

Certainly these demands reflected explicitly the fears of the Northern elites and a desire, genuine or not, to see closer relations between the North and South. Furthermore, the Northern suspicions were aroused when, upon the Northern request to participate in administration of the country, the government declared in 1944 the establishment of Advisory Council for the Northern Sudan. In this Council, the Southern Sudan was not represented. Thus, when the Northern Sudan Advisory Council was inaugurated in May 1944, its most visible defeat was the exclusion of any representation from the South. Moreover, the councilors were prohibited to discuss or to speak on matters related to the Southern part of the country.[48]

By the end of the Second World War, there emerged a growing collective 'guilt' in the Sudan political service that they had done a little to the South. To many of them the adoption and the implementation of the Southern policy was drastic failure.

As early as 1940 for example, voices were heard talking

about possible unity of the South to the North as a symptom of the Southern policy failure. According to one official, the political future of the Southern Sudan, can not yet be determined but whatever it may be:

> "... *we should work a scheme toward self-government which would fit an ultimate attachment of the Southern Sudan peoples Southward (Uganda or East Africa) or Northward (Northern Sudan); and can not be excluded if we admit the principle of self-determination, but the policy that being adopted makes political adhesion to the North improbable from the Southern point of view.*"[49]

By 1945, tendency towards abrogation of the 1930 Southern policy started to preoccupy discussions among the government officials. Views supporting possibility of formulating a workable Southern policy were circulated in private correspondences of those officials directly involved in Southern affairs. Some went as expressing their views in a negative, defensive and sometimes conservative manner; one of these officials was quoted as saying:

> "... *while the British might in due course be in position to grant self-government in the North, the difficulty would be to safeguard the very large Negroid element, which has never progressed and presumably never will*".[50]

In fact, once the British officials in Khartoum regarded the South as a remote alien territory, they began, out of ignorance of the region perhaps, to treat it like a foreign land, distinct and separate. This might be because they seemed to have deceived themselves that a political decision need not accompany an economic decision. i.e. issuing a dozen of orders, formulating Southern policy without providing needed funds to implement them. The irony in this process was that, to develop the South to enable its people to determine their future relationship with North, eliminated, as time passed, and unintentionally perhaps every alternative but union.[51]

In other words, the government policy on the South, as we have seen in 1920's seemed to have produced the condition to have no choice other than unity with the north, but why?

In August 4th, 1945 the Sudan Governor-General dispatched a memorandum to the High Commissioner in Cairo in which he forwarded three alternatives for the future of the South:

- Integration of the South to the North,
- Integration of the South into East Africa *or*
- Integrating of the parts of the south with the North and other parts in Equatoria with East Africa.

However, the idea of attaching the South or parts of it to East Africa was not in any case entertained by the Southern tribes. They did not want to display any wish to rush into the unwelcome arms of their neighbors with whom they had long-standing rivalry. Moreover, Kenya and Uganda were British colonies with different status than the Sudan, a fact well known to the chiefs and the half educated Southerners, let alone the 'Bog Barons', another name for the British Southern administrators.

On the other hand, the East African authorities themselves gave no encouragement for any link with the Southern Sudan. Thus, since the British officials in East Africa did not want the Southern Sudan, the Sudan government no longer had concern about any external pressure for the idea of the South attachment to East Africa. However, the idea was considered by the Northern Sudanese positive step since it suggested a revision of and reversal of the 1930 Southern policy. On the other hand, the Egyptians made it clear that they want Sudan to be incorporated into their kingdom; and unlike Southern Sudanese disinterest in East Africa, the Northern Sudanese kept up a constant propaganda and demands for the union of the Nile Valley with Egypt.

It is to be recalled that by the end of the Second World War, all the Northern political groups were able to organize themselves into political parties. Moreover, the tribal makeup of the Northern Sudanese was by the turn of the 20th century diluted by the concept of Northern Sudanese Nationalism and the religious cohesiveness in the North. However, the problem of coming to terms with social heterogeneity were much clear in the South which was not involved in the development of political parties in the country.[52] This was reflected by the differences in the South, mainly the lack of building of a political relation between state and society in the South itself. It was also reflected in the lack of social and economic development of the South. However, the most important reason was the lack of modern institutions such as commercial groups or trade unions, all of which would have raised political consciousness.

In other words, an awareness of national politics would probably not have emerged in the South after the Second World War if it had not been that party politics were taking place in the North. In fact, it was the constitutional responses to the northern parties on the part of the Sudan government that injected, if one may say, political awareness into the South. This lack of awareness in the South was used by the Civil Secretary as partially responsible for the necessity of reversing the Southern policy of 1930.

In a memorandum to the Southern governors in May 1946 in which he explained the difficulty of finding political elite to represent Southern view, James Robertson went on to say:

> *"Although it was difficult to see how the Southern representatives could play a part in an extended advisory council, there was no possibility now of separating. If the next twenty years the Southern Sudan has not progressed to stand on its own feet in the independent (corrected by hand to 'self-governing') Sudan, it may be necessary to make some temporary arrangements to ensure the interests of the inhabitants until they are able to play an equal part ... it is obvious that the South will probably require the assistance of non-Sudanese for a*

considerable time after the Northern Sudan has
dispensed with them."[53]

The change that took place in the Civil Secretary's traditional view can only be explained if, among other things, we consider external and internal factors that made such turn around possible in 1946.

External Factors

There was no doubt that the post Second World War has weaken the British imperial hegemony and power in the world with the consequent change in its colonial policy and practices. In fact some of the prominent features of these weaknesses included:

- The United States assumed the leadership, being a British ally in the war and in the North Atlantic Treaty Organization (NATO) in the West as the 'Cold war' era set in.
- The United States policy of 'containment' of what used to be USSR, particularly in the Middle East and North Africa.
- The Egyptian pressure on Britain to withdraw its troops from Egyptian territory was growing, the US policy of containment in the Middle East and the British desperate need to maintain the strategic importance of the Suez Canal Zone; all of these made Britain more serious to make a compromise with Egypt on this issue.

The British government was forced to seek an agreement on the Sudan as well as to satisfy the demands of the Northern Sudanese without antagonizing Egypt.[54]

The question of maintenance of a British military base in

the Canal Zone came on the surface when in December 1945 Egypt requested Britain to initiate a conference to revise the Anglo-Egyptian treaty of 1936 both in regard to the presence of British troops in the Canal Zone and the Future status of the Sudan. In the negotiations that followed, the Egyptian Prime Minister Sidgi Pasha and British Secretary for Foreign Affairs, Ernest Bevin, concluded and agreement 'Sidgi-Bevin Agreement' which provided for the evacuation of the British troops from Egypt within three years.

The Agreement failed however; because in a "Draft Sudan Protocol" a disagreement occurred on the interpretation. It was after that failure that the Sudan Administration Conference (SAC) was initiated. Another reason for the reversal of Southern policy was that the British feared that the Egyptians would raise the case of Sudan status, hence the internationalization of the Southern Sudan future, before the Untied Nations.[55]

Internal Factors

The internal pressures were equally hard on the British government as were the external factors. Some of the internal factors, which forced the British government to reverse its 1930 southern Policy included:

Egyptian pressure on Britain to evacuate Sudan to revert to Egypt of historical right.

The pressure of the 'Sudanese nationalists' for self-rule. In April 1946 the pro-independence political groups, led by the Umma Party, together with members of Advisory Council for the Northern Sudan, requested the Governor-General for the conference to study and to recommend to him provisions for institutions and other means to speed up devolution.[56] The Conference was convened as requested on April 22, 1946. The first meetings held on 24-25 April, set up two sub-committees; the first subcommittee contained recommendations for closer association of the Sudanese with central government. The second committee considered the relations between the North and the South. After the conference deliberations, a joint report was issued and submitted to the Governor-General Council for consideration and approval. The question of the association of the South Sudan in the proposed 'central institutions' was incorporated in the recommendations for the establishment of a central 'Legislative assembly'. The report made it clear that the members of the conference insisted that the proposed assembly should represent the whole country.

According to the SAC's members, Southern Sudanese have to be administered as an integral part of the whole Sudan and they are to participate in the Central Legislative Assembly and the obstacles to social and economic exchange within the country were to be abolished.[57]

In the final analysis, it seems plausible to say that the external factors, especially the one regarding Egyptian pressure, culminated in pressurizing Britain to speed up the process of developing administrative and political power to the hands of the Northern Sudanese in "Central Institution". Yet, it appeared that both the external and internal factors combined were directed to oppose the isolation of the South from North. The above steps were the tools through which the

THE IDEA OF SOUTH SUDAN

abandonment of the Southern Policy of 1930 was carried out.[58]

Equipped with the above background, the Civil Secretary, Sir James Robertson, issued a memorandum dated December 16th, 1946 addressed to the British administrators in the South, using the Khartoum secret dispatch of August 4, 1945, as the base of reference. In his memo, Robertson declared that:

> *"... we should now work on the assumption that the Sudan, as at present constituted, with possibly minor boundary adjustment, will remain one."*[59]

He added that we should therefore restate our Southern Policy and do so publicly as follows:

> *"The policy of the Sudan government regarding the Southern Sudan is to act upon the facts that the peoples of the Southern Sudan are distinctly African and Negroid but that geography and economics combined, so far as can be foreseen at the future development to the Middle Eastern and Arabicized Northern Sudan."*[60]

As to the method through which the new policy will be implemented, the Civil Secretary went on the explain that:

> *"to ensure that the peoples of the South shall by educational and economic development be equipped*

to stand up for themselves in the future as socially
and economically the equals of their partners of the
Northern Sudan in the Sudan of the future."[61]

The Civil Secretary reminded his administrators in the South that 'Great changes' had occurred and the 'Sudanization' in the North could be accelerated, regardless of the outcome of Anglo-Egyptian negotiations; likewise the public discussion of the 'Southern Sudan question' should be brought to light.

The new policy, he advised them, must command the support of Northern Sudanese and relieve the doubts of the British officials. He stressed that plans for better communication between the South and East Africa had become to nothing.

On education, the new policy stipulated that Southerners must look to Gordon College for post-secondary schooling; and Arabic should be taught in the South from intermediate level upwards. The memorandum went on to recommend that distinctions in pay and conditions of employment, attempts at economic separations, and other differences were more and more abnormal as the South's isolation broke down.[62]

Robertson closed his letter by stressing that 'urgency' was the essence of the problem:

"We no longer have time to aim at the ideal, we
must aim at doing what is the best for the Southern

peoples in the present circumstances."[63]

Reactions to the 1946 Memorandum on the Southern Policy

The British administrators in the South
In general terms, the reactions of the administrators in the South to the new policy were varied. While some favored it, others disagreed and questioned the logic on which it was based.

Among the first administrators to react to the Civil Secretary memo was B.B. Marwood, the Governor of Equatoria. While admitting his agreement with the new policy, Marwood proposed to press for 'safeguards' and period of 'trusteeship' till the South is vocal and knows what he called 'its own mind". In his opinion and as price to this new policy:

> *"... the North must accept to pay the bill of this policy to develop the south and be capable of depending this policy to develop the South and be capable of depending this policy by sound argument."*[64]

Governor Marwood was keen to show that, although this policy was necessary, it was short of unwillingness of the northerners to admit racial differences between the two parts. These differences, in his view, necessitated British interference by providing safeguards to the Southerners, in whose behalf until then, the British administrators were talking.

J.H. Wilson, the District Commissioner of Jur River District, agreed in principle with the new policy, but felt that time was not yet conducive for the South to be left alone. Instead, he was with the opinion that the best *"future the British could give to the South is Federation with the North on equal footing"*.[65] In fact, he was against what he called *"clouding the unification of the two parts by vague promises of self-determination in the South."*[66]

This promise, he believed, would antagonize Northern opinion and will raise false hopes in the South. The correct policy, he argued, was for the British to take over the trustee-ship of one united Sudan and as one united Sudan the British should hand it back to a government of equal Northern and Southern Sudan. He concluded by pointing out that 'educated Southern' opinion must be taken into consideration when formulating a policy. He argued that they were discontented with their conditions of service and considered that the government has let the South down; these people he said:

> *"... unless nursed carefully will be a source of trou-*
> *ble in the future when their numbers increase and*
> *their opinion and actions are concerted."*[67]

Mr. T.R. Owen, District Commissioner of Rembeck, like Wilson, was in favour of a period of trusteeship. During this time the Southern affairs could be administered by a council consisting of the Civil Secretary, the Southern Governors and two members, one from the South and other from North, the last two were to be nominated by the Governor-General.

However, Mr. Owen believed that the Northern Sudanese

were not fit to administer the South, because, as he put it,

> *"that Northern Sudanese could run Omdurman*
> *I believe; that they will soon be fit to govern the*
> *Rezaigat and Hadendawa is possible; that they will*
> *in next two decades (1946-1956) be entrusted with*
> *the Azande is even unthinkable."*[68]

In his response to the civil secretary, Owen recommended that assurances should be given that the British administrators would remain in the South and see to it that the South would not be dominated by an Arab civilization in Khartoum, which is alien to them.

When the minutes of the Sudan Administration Conference (SAC) were published, six British administrators in the South signed a letter and sent it to the Civil Secretary expressing their dissatisfaction with the recommendations. In their response, the administrators stressed that these minutes:

> *"... have given the impression that the future of*
> *the South is being discussed by the wrong people*
> *in the wrong place, hence the government's deci-*
> *sion is likely to be thereby directed into wrong*
> *channels."*[69]

They further noted that no Southern Sudanese was present in the SAC and there was no serious effort made to extract the opinion of the 'enlightened or leading' Southerners themselves. The six signatories did not believe that any proposal

made for Southern representation in an assembly at the capital would amount to full representation that could guard the
interests of Southern provinces.

Instead, the six administrators called for a separate admin-
istrative conference for the Southern Sudan to meet in the
South, composed of Civil Secretary, representative of Legal
Department, the two Southern governors, not less than three
Northern Sudanese and not less than ten Southern Sudanese
to be selected by the governors.[70]

Furthermore, the six signatories suggested the following
proposals for Southern policy:
1. That the government policy must be based on the assump-
   tion that the Sudan remains one country;
2. They stressed that the two halves are different in race,
   tradition, language, customs and outlook;
3. As such they have got to be treated distinctly and regarded
   as partners.

The prerequisite in their opinion to that, unless this
distinction and partnership is allowed, wholesome political
development of the Southern Sudan is impossible. While they
deemed speeding up of local development in the South as an
urgent political need, they suggested that during this preparation period, Southern Sudan Advisory Council should be
formed. The objective of this Southern advisory Council is to
lead to a single Legislative Assembly for the whole country, in
which conscious, full and sufficient Southern representation
will be assured.[71]

In fact, the intention of the proposals seemed to have been

for an alternative approach to the political future of the South. These proposals were to form the frame of what later become known as 'Juba conference'. In other words, the six signatories or the 'the six British rebels as they were nicknamed, accepted regionalism or federation as the only correct policy, which would protect the interests of the South.

The Reaction of Northern Sudanese

The Northern Sudanese reaction to the December 16, 1946 memorandum is fully reflected in the Sudan Administration Conference minutes of January 8th, 1946. Based on these minutes, the Northern parties recommended that the Governor-General, among other things, should cancel unconditionally all the restrictions that were obstacles toward the North-South unity. They further demanded that an All-Sudan Legislative Assembly should be established in which both South and the North would be represented.

The Civil Secretary memorandum was therefore, in consistent with the Northern Sudanese demands. Hence, their reaction was wholly in favor of the abandonment of 1930 Southern policy. Moreover, they considered the British administrators' demand for safeguards in return for the Southern Sudanese participation as nothing, but a negative response that was put forward to hinder the unity of the country. In their opinion, the British were presenting their own views, since 'Southern Sudan' as entity did not have up to that time a united "political opinion" on what was taking place in the country.[72]

To North Sudanese, there was no 'Southern Sudan' as a political entity to be represented in any political forum where national issues were discussed. The Southern absence in the Sudan Administration Conference was therefore justified on the ground that there was no organized Southern Political opinion.

Southern Sudanese reaction

The December 1946 memorandum was as far as the Southern Sudanese people were concerned not different from the 1930 policy. This was because, first, both policies were initiated, approved, and in the case of the first one, implemented without Southern participation. Second, it has become a tradition that whenever the central government decides to change or implement any policy related to Southern Sudan, directives were addressed to and carried out by the governors of Southern provinces.[73]

The British, as mentioned earlier, had fought to prevent the creation of intelligentsia like the one existed in the North. Consequently, there was only handful of junior clerical staff, who, only often complained about their positions. In 1946, 73 South staff signed a letter complaining about their conditions in which they remarked:

> *"... we cannot understand what the government means by saying that we are different from the Northern Sudanese, although we are all Sudanese. This assertion may be attributed admittedly to*

our backwardness, and if so the fault lies with the
Government."[74]

However, these complaints, though revealing, did not constitute a major political development; the small number of these
civil servants were largely isolated from the tribes where they
come from, and there was no sign that through this group
much would emerge. The concept of a "Southern Sudan" as a
separate entity did not, at the time of their complaint, have a
political significance. For them, Southern Sudan was person-
ified in the three Southern governors. In fact, they considered
themselves as civil servants serving the Sudan government
like their counterparts in the North. Instead, they identify
themselves as Bari, Nuers, Shilluks or Azande inhabitants of
a country called 'Sudan'.

In response to the demands of the British administrators
in the South and pressurized by the Northern Sudanese,
and in order to seek views of the 'Southern Sudanese', the
Civil Secretary agreed to hold the proposed 'Administrative
Conference' in the Southern Sudan. In his opinion:

"... to rule out Southern participation in the
proposed Legislative Assembly would be viewed with
great disappointment by the Northern Sudan and
would incline many of those who now are supporters
of the Sudan government to go into opposition and
drift across to the Egyptian side."[75]

It was therefore, through the above series of reactions and

background that the new Southern policy of 1946 came about; hence the Juba meeting of June 1947.

The Juba Conference

The Civil Secretary moved quickly to defuse the tension in the South. He agreed to call a conference in Juba in June 1947, by leaving the terms of reference and the selection of the Southern Sudanese representatives to his critics, the three governors in the South. It took the Administration Conference ten months to decide upon proposals for Legislative Assembly, but took Robertson less than three months to consult southerners.[76] The meting was held on June 12 and 13, 1947 in Juba cinema. At conference, Sudan government was represented by Robertson, Marwood, Kingdon, and Owen. The Northern Sudanese representatives were Ibrahim Badri, Dr. Habib Abdallah Shaykh Surur Mahmmed Ramli, Hasan Ahmed Uthman and Mohammad Salih Shangeiti. Seventeen Southerners were selected, including some who later on were to play an active part in the Southern Sudan affairs – Phelimon Majok, Clement Mboro, James Tembura, Both Diu, Chief Lolik Lado, Siricio Iro, Edward Adhok, Lueth Ajak, Kunyangi Ababa, Hassan Fertak, Chief Cir Rehan, Chief Gir Kiro, Pastor Andrea Apaya, Chief Ukuma Bazia, Chief Lappanya, Father Guido Akou, and Chief Tete.[77]

Moreover, there was no formal agenda for the conference rather Robertson had prepared a detailed terms of reference to guide deliberations. The meeting was to discuss:

1. Recommendations made by SAC about the South;
2. The advisability of the Southern Sudanese being

THE IDEA OF SOUTH SUDAN

represented in the proposed Legislative Assembly;

3. Whether safeguards could be introduced to ensure that South was not hindered in its social and political advancement;

4) Whether separate Southern Advisory Council should be created;

5) Other matters not strictly administrative, which the SAC had considered essential for unifying the Sudanese.78

The conference was opened by the Chairman and had had difficulty explaining the changes that were taking place both in the North and in the South.

On the first day of the conference on June 12th, 1947, Southern delegates took a stand that they were not yet prepared, for the lack of experience, to take part in the proposed Assembly. Instead, they wanted to have an Advisory Council of their own, in the same way as the North had; this will be a means of preparing them to participate in the Central Assembly.

The Northern Sudanese delegates to the Conference opposed the idea of an advisory Council for the South, since based on their own interpretation, it meant separation of the South from the North. The parties continued in the first day to insist on their views.79

On the second day no serious discussions took place, rather, the Civil Secretary made a concluding Summary statement that:

"there seemed to have been a change of mind among

the Southern members, but that the discussion had
been a useful one."[80]

In other words, it seemed that some of the 'educated
Southerners' changed their minds from the previous day and
argued that the Southerners could only protect themselves by
participating in the Legislative Assembly in Khartoum.

As James Tembura put it:

"Judge Shengeiti had said that if we did not partic-
ipate we will have no say in the future government
of the Sudan."[81]

That was the end of the famous 'Juba Conference'. In fact M.
F. Keen, Secretary to the Juba Conference, expressed in relief
that:

"if the Southerners had said they did not want to
go with the North, we would not really have known
what to do with the South."[82]

The Civil Secretary, James Robertson, on the other hand,
summed up his views in a note to the Governor-General's
Council by stating that in his opinion:

"... the South must be administered as an inte-
gral part of the Sudan – the legislative Assembly
and the Executive Council should legislate for the
whole country, but powers should reserve to the

Governor-General in cases where Legislation or administrative order appears to him to have unfortunate results in the South,"[83] in order that its actions should be suspended.

In the final analysis, the Northern politicians were pleased with the outcome of the meeting, for to them, the meeting was a historical landmark for the national unity. On the other hand, the British administrators in the South felt betrayed. On his part, Robertson had two limited objectives both achieved by the speed with which he acted to the protestations of the southern administrators: first, was his symbolic solicitation of Southern opinion and he wanted to make up for the omission of Southerners in any discussions of future governance in the Sudan.[84]

The Southern delegates to the Juba Conference felt that their presence had 'a special' historical meeting because:

They regarded the conference as the only occasion that the South as an entity was invited to a forum where its representatives were nominally allowed to decide their fate.

For the first time in the Condominium's history the British administrators in the South permitted to lift their 'protective isolation' of the South politically and geographically.

Southern delegates did not come to Juba as tribal representatives rather they attended as delegates of 'Southern people.'[85] Their presence as such can be considered as the first active Southern participation in a united Sudan politics. They were there to speak for the South.

Practically, the Juba Conference resulted in that the Southern policy of 1930 was completely reversed. Borders between the two regions were reopened, religious freedom was extended to all religions; salaries and wages were equalized, but little was done on the social and economic development in the South.

On the legal plane, the nature of the Juba Conference, as the Governor of Equatoria put it, "was explanatory only and no decisions, binding or otherwise, were taken; the two delegates were there to learn each other's ideas". [86]

Moreover, the proceedings of the conference were neither officially published nor made public. To prove the last point, James Robertson endorsed later the fact that the 'Juba conference' as he preferred to call it, was not a continuation of the Sudan Administration Conference. He confidently insisted that:

> " ... *the only decision resulting from the Conference was taken by myself. I decided that I could, after what I had seen of the Southerners who attended, endorse the recommendations of the Administrative Conference and asked the Governor-General in Council to accept its proposal that new Legislative Assembly should be representative of the whole Sudan.*"[87]

On the whole, the important element that requires emphasis regarding the outcome of Juba Conference is that it represented the final result of the first two attempts made by the Sudan government to find a 'suitable' policy for the Southern Sudan. Sir Robertson's decision to call the Juba Conference was not a reaction to the 'British Southern rebels,' but a last trial, to use their concerns to strengthen the Sudan government's position against Cairo, London and Northern Sudanese vis-à-vis the unorganized Southern political opinion.[88]

Southern Sudan was represented in the conference by chiefs, clerks, teachers and clerics. In fact, it was these groups who were in later years to provide the 'emergence of the Southern consciousness"; it was this group among whom a 'sentiment of Southern Communalism' was to develop.[89]

Therefore, the emergence of Southern political conscious-ness, as we shall elaborate later, was in response to the character of the emerging Sudan than as a political awaken-ing. In fact, the emergence of the Southern politicians did not yet mark the first incorporation of the South as a whole into Sudanese national politics. In the final analysis, the signif-icance of the Juba Conference in June 1947 lies in that, the South was represented, for the first time, by individuals who considered themselves as 'Southern Sudanese'.[90] In a word, a landmark on new Southern politics was born, and therefore 'Southern awareness' began from then on to shape itself.

End Notes

1   The Anglo-Egyptian Agreement of 1899 in Muddathir Abd Al Rahim's *Imperialism and Nationalism in the Sudan: A Study in Constitutional and Political Development, 1899-1956* (Oxford: The Clarendon press, 1969), pp.233-36; Peter Malcolm Holt, *A History of the Sudan: From Coming of Islam to the Present Day* (London: Longman Group UK Limited, 1988) pp. 117-52.

2   Martin W. Daly, *Empire on the Nile; The Anglo-Egyptian Sudan 1898-1934* (Cambridge: Cambridge University Press, 1986), pp. 396-403; K.D.D. Henderson, Sudan Republic (London: Ernest Been Limited, 1965), p. 160.

3   Robert O. Collins, *Shadows in the Grass: Britain in the Southern Sudan, 1918-1956* (New Haven: Yale University press, 1983), pp. 3-41.

4   John R. Ducan, *The Sudan: A Record of Achievement* (Edinburgh: William Blackwood & Sons Ltd., 1952), pp. 99-101; Robert O. Collins, *Land Beyond The Rivers: The Southern Sudan, 1898-1918* (New Haven, Yale University press, 1971), p. 164.

5   H. Stignand, *Administration in Tropical Africa* (London, 1914), p. 34.

6   Daly, *Empire on the Nile*, p. 142 pp.136-7.

7   Peter Woodward, *Sudan, 1898-1989: The Unstable State* (Boulder: Lynne Rienner Publishers, 1990), p. 25; H.C. Jackson, *Behind The Modern Sudan* (London: MacMillian & Co. Ltd., 1955), pp.61-5.

8   Arfaf Abdel Majid Abu Hasabu, *Factional Conflict in the Sudanese Nationalist Movement 1918-1948* Khartoum: University of Khartoum press, 1985), pp.7-9; Daly, Empire on the Nile, pp.138-39.

9   *Sudan: A country Study* (Washington D.C.: Foreign Area Studies, 1982), pp. 36-41; Jackson, *Behind The Modern Sudan*, pp. 86-7.

10 Daly, *Empire on the Nile*, p. 143.

11 Great Britain, Parliament, *Parliamentary Debates* House of Commons) vol. 52 (January 31 – Dec. 16, 911), p. 375.

12 Muddathir Abd Al Rahim, "The Development of British Policy in the Southern Sudan" *Middle Eastern Studies* 2, No 3 (1966), pp. 227-49; Robert O. Collins, "The Aliab Uprising and its Suppression" *Sudan Notes and Records* 48 (1967), pp. 77-89.

13 G. Lienhardt, "The Sudan: Aspects of the South Government among some of the Nilotec peoples, 1947-52" *British Society for Middle Eastern Studies Bulletin* 9; (1982), pp. 22-34; Daly, Empire on the Nile, pp. 137-9.

14 John R. Ducan, *The Sudan's Path to Independence* (Edinburgh; Blackwoo, 1957), pp. 57-114; Lienhardt, "The Sudan: Aspects of the South Government - - - -", pp. 24-30.

15 Great Britain, Parliament, *Parliamentary Debates* (House of Commons) vol. 227 (6 Nov. 1928-May 10, 1929), p. 1743; Collins, *Land Beyond The Rivers*, pp. 199-203.

16 Great Britain, Parliament, *Parliamentary Debates* (House of Commons) vol. 43 (Feb. 14, 1912-March 7, 1913), p. 421; J. Jackson, *Behind the Modern Sudan* pp. 140-58

17 H.C. Jackson, *Sudan Days and Ways* (London: MacMillan & Co. Ltd., 1954), pp. 138-70); Great Britain, Parliament, *Parliamentary Debates* (House of Commons), vol. 37 (Feb. 14, 1912-March, 7, 1913) p. 9; Collins, *Shadows in the Grass*, pp. 38-41.

18 Great Britain, parliament, *Parliamentary Debates* (House of Commons), Vol. 43 (Feb. 14, 1912-March 7, 1913), p. 421; Sir Harold Macmichael, *The Sudan*, (London: Ernest Benn Limited, 1954), pp. 91-101.

19 Daly, *Empire on the Nile*, pp. 403-4

20 Collins, *Shadows in the Grass*, pp. 29-37.

21 *The Sudan: A Record of Progress, 1898-1947* (Printed by the authority of Sudan Government, 1947), pp.12-14; Collins, Shadows in the Grass, pp. 25-8.

22 Daly, *Empire on the Nile*; P. 148; also Collins, *Shadows in the Grass*, pp.35-112; These pages discuss in length the difficulties the government encountered to implement its 1930 Southern policy.

23 Muhammad O. Beshir, *Southern Sudan: Background to Conflict* (Khartoum" Khartoum University press, 1968), pp. 37-8; Also George W. Shephard, "National Integration and the Southern Sudan", *The Journal of Modern African Studies*, 4, No. 2 (1966), pp. 193-212.

24 Beshir, *The Southern Sudan: Background to Conflict*, p. 40.

25 Daly, *Empire on the Nile*, p. 148.

26 Beshir, *Southern Sudan: Background to Conflict*, p. 41.

27 Lienhardt, "The Sudan: Aspects of the South Government among ...", pp. 22-34.

28 Ducan, *The Sudan*, p. 100; Abd Al-Rahim, "The Development of British Southern Policy ...", pp. 223-27.

29 Holt, A History of the Sudan ..., p. 139; Bshir, *Southern Sudan; Background to Conflict*, pp. 40-42.

30 Beshir, *Southern Sudan: Background to Conflict*, p. 42.

31 Collins, *Shadows in the Grass*, p. 59.

32 Daly, *Empire on the Nile*, p. 405.

33 *Sudan Gazette*, No. 402, October 15, 1922.

34 Daly, *Empire on the Nile*, p. 407.

35 Behir, *Southern Sudan: Background to Conflict*, pp. 115-18.

36 Dustan M. Wai, ed. *The Southern Sudan and the Problem National Integration* (London: Frank Cass, 1973(, p. 15.

37 S.M. Sid Ahmed, "Christian Missionary Activities in Sudan 1926-1948" in *Southern Sudan: Religionalism and Religion*, edited by Mohammed O. Beshir (Khartoum: University of Khartoum press, 1984), pp. 241-76; also see R. Hill, "Government and Christian Missions in the Anglo-Egyptian Sudan, 1899-1914" *Middle Eastern Studies*, 1 (January 1965), pp. 113-34.

38 Abd Al Rahim *Imperialism and Nationalism in the Sudan*, pp. 75-9; also Abd al Rahim, "The Development of British policy in Southern Sudan, 1899-1947", pp.227-49.

39 Beshir, *Southern Sudan; Background to Conflict*, p. 59.

40 Collins, *Shadows in the Grass*, pp.270-73.

41 Daly, *Empire on the Nile*, p. 412.

42 Collins, *Shadows in the Grass*, pp. 173-98.

43 1930 Memorandum on the Southern policy in Beshir's *Southern Sudan: Background to Conflict*, pp. 115-18; Henderson, Sudan Republic, pp. 161-66.

44 For more elaboration on this point see the Full text of MacMichael's letter to the three governors on May 10, 1928 in Collin's *Shadows in the Grass*, p. 172.

45 Beshir, 1930 Memorandum on Southern policy, pp. 115-18; Abd Al Rahim, "The Development of British Policy in Southern Sudan, 1899-1947", pp.227-249.

46 John Obert Voll and Sarah Potts Vol. *The Sudan: Unity and Diversity in Multi-Cultural State* (Boulder: West View Press, 1985). pp. 57-8.

47 Robert O. Collins, "Sudanese Nationalism, Southern Policy and the Unification of the Sudan, 1939-1949" in *The Nationalist Movement in the Sudan* edited by Mahasin Abdel Gadir Hag al-Safi (Khartoum: University of Khartoum press, 1989), pp. 222-265.

48 Woodward, *Sudan, 1898-1989: The Unstable State*, pp. 71-2.

49 Peter Woodward, "The South in Sudanese Politics, 1946-1956", *Middle Eastern Studies*, 16, No, 3 (1980), pp. 178-92.

50 Ibid., pp. 180-82.

51 Collins, "Sudanese Nationalism, Southern Policy and Unification of the Sudan, 1939-1946", pp. 225-26

52 Bashir, *Southern Sudan: Background to Conflict*, p. 63.

53 Martin W. Daly, *Imperial Sudan: The Anglo-Egyptian Condominium, 1934-1956*, (Cambridge: Cambridge University press, 1991), pp.234-42; Abdel Alier, *Southern Sudan: Too Many Agreements Dishonoured*, (Exter: Ithaca press, 1990), pp.13-23.

54 Henderson, *Sudan Republic*, pp.164-5.

55 Abu Hasabu, *Factional Conflict in the Sudanese Nationalist Movement 1918-1948*, pp. 139-49; also see Collins, "Sudanese Nationalism, Southern Policy and the Unification of the Sudan, 1939-46", pp. 232-34.

56 Great Britain, Parliament, *Sessional Papers* (House of Commons) "Report on Administration of the Sudan for the Year 1948", 1950-51, CMD. 8181 Vol. XIX, p.817.

57 Richard Gray, "The Southern Sudan" *Journal of Contemporary History* 6 (1971), pp. 108-20.

58 Daly, *Imperial Sudan*, p. 236.

59 Anglo Lobale Loiria, "The Juba Conference: A Critical Appraisal" in *The Nationalist Movements* in the *Sudan*, edited by Mahasin Abdel Sadir Haj al-Safi (Khartoum: University of Khartoum press `989), pp. 266-94.

60 Ibid., pp. 288-9.

61 Holt, *A History of the Sudan*, p. 153.

62 Abu Hasabu, *Factional Conflict in the Sudanese Nationalist Movement, 1918-1948*, p. 143.

63 Oliber Albino, *The Sudan:A Southern Viewpoint* (Oxford: Oxford University press, 1970), p.22.

64 1946 Memorandum on Southern policy, Khartoum, December 1946, in Mohammad O.Beshir's *Southern Sudan: Background to Conflict*, pp. 119-21.

65 Ibid., p. 120

66 Daly, *Imperial Sudan*, p. 237.

67 Abd Al-Rahim, *Imperialism and Nationalism in the Sudan, 1899-1956*, pp.166-72.

68 Albino, *The Sudan: A Southern Point*, p. 24.

69 Governor Equatoria Reacts to Southern Policy of 1946, Juba, December 23, 1946 in Beshir's *Southern Sudan: Background to Conflict*, pp.122-23.

70 Further reactions to 1946 Southern policy, Wau, March 10, 1947, in Beshir's *Southern Sudan: Background to Conflict*, pp.134-43.

71 Daly, *Imperial Sudan*, p.238.

72 Further reactions to 1946 Southern policy, Wau, March 10, 1947, p. 135.

73 F.R.H. Own's Reaction to 1946 Southern Policy, January 5, 1946 in Beshir's *Southern Sudan Background to Conflict*, pp. 127-29.

74 District Commissioner Rumbek's Reaction to 1946 Southern Policy, Rumbek, January 29, 1947, in Beshir, *Southern Sudan Background to Conflict*, pp. 130-31; Collins, *Shadows in the Grass*, pp. 285-92.

75 Daly, *Imperial Sudan*, p. 237.

76 Collins, "Sudanese Nationalism, Southern Policy and the Unification of the Sudan, 1939-1946", pp. 258-59.

77 Abu Hasabu, *Factional Conflict in the Sudanese Nationalist Movement 1918-1948*, pp. 146-49.

78 Woodward, "The South in Sudanese Politics, 1946-1956", pp. 178-92.

79 Collins, *Shadows in the Grass*, p. 272.

80 Abdel Alier, "The Southern Sudan Question", in *The Southern Sudan and the Problem of National Integration*, edited by Dustan M. Wai (London: Frank Cass, 1973), pp. 9-27.

81 Joseph Oduho, *The Problem of Southern Sudan*, (London: Oxford University press, 1963), pp. 13-20.

82 Proceedings of the Juba Conference on the political development of the Southern Sudan, Juba, June 12-13, 1947 in Beshir's *The Southern Sudan: Background to Conflict*, pp. 136-53.

83 Ibid., p. 138.

84 Peter Russell and Storrs MacCall, "Can Succession be Justified? The case of the Southern Sudan" *The Southern Sudan and the Problem of National Integration*, pp. 93-119.

85 Ibid., 93-119

86 Loiria, "The Juba Conference: A Critical Appraisal," pp. 270-80.

87 Collins, *Shadows in the Grass*, p. 291.

88 Ibid., p. 292.

89 Albino, *The Sudan: A Southern Viewpoint*, pp. 25-8; Alier, "The Southern Sudan Question," pp. 16-8; Woodward, "The South in Sudanese Politics, 1946-1956," p. 183; Gray, "The Southern Sudan," p. 115; Daly, *Imperial Sudan*, pp. 241-2; Collins, *Shadows in the Grass*, pp. 138-92, Loiria, "The Juba Conference", pp. 278-80; Loiria, "The Juba Conference: A Critical Appraisal," pp.. 278-80; Woodward, *Sudan, 1898-1989*, p. 72.; Loiria, "Juba conference – ", pp. 267-93. It was from this meeting on that we can talk about 'Southern groups, interest groups, and Southern opinion'.

CHAPTER TWO

The Development of the Southern Sudanese Political Groups, 1948 – 1957

~

O nce Southerners reluctantly accepted the creation of an all-Sudan Legislative Assembly, the question of 'safeguards' for the South came on surface. Sir James Robertson suggested that in order to resolve the Southern concern:

> *"... the Governor-General Should be specifically empowered to suspend the application of any law in the South or to specify conditions for its application."*[1]

On the other hand, the Northern Sudanese rejected any specific reference to the Southern Sudan. The British administrators in the South argued that these safeguards were important to the South and should be specifically and boldly stated. Meanwhile, the Egyptians openly opposed any special treatment of the South. The result of this row was an agreement between the British, Egyptians and the Northern Sudanese that no specific reference should be made to Southern Sudan. Their argument was that the Governor-General's powers, as they stood under the Agreement of 1899, were sufficient enough to suspend any law of the Assembly.[2]

As discussed earlier, the purpose of the new Legislative Assembly was to govern a united North and South under a centralized government. The difficulty of selecting new members to represent the South in the Legislative Assembly became a daunting task for some administrators in the South.

Part of the difficulty was that there was no organized political party in the South at the time, let alone an organize interest group. Moreover, establishment of institutions in the South had not progressed to a point where any person or group could claim to represent Southern interests in a political forum. The third issue was the difficulty faced by governors to persuade individuals to go to the Khartoum.

In Upper Nile province, for instance, F. D. Corfield, found it difficult to persuade any of his head chiefs to go to Khartoum since all government officials who would like to join Legislative Assembly must leave their jobs. He was lucky to find among the provincial councilors four reluctant representatives to go to north. The nominees were Al-Hajj Muhamed Abdulla, a northerner; Both Diu, a Nuer chief; Lual Dengkak, a Dinka; and Edward Adhok, a Shiluk chief.[3]

In Bahr al-Ghazal province the nomination was rather easier. The Governor nominated five representatives to fill in the seats allocated to his province. They were Stanslaus Paysama, administrative officer; Cir Rihan, Twic Dinka Chief; Abdulla Majok, retired Sergeant Major, Sudanese Defense Force; and Khamis Mursal Ashugul, a store keeper in Wau.

In Equatoria, representatives were easy to be selected. They were: Andrea Gore, Bari from Tombur, Juba District; Banjamin Lwoki, teacher, Yei; Korokongwa Hassan, Moru chief, Amadi; Sincio Iro, Former administrative assistant, Torit; and Yona Kaka, Yambio.[4] Later on, James Tembura was made member as a nominee of the Governor-General, since he was ahead clerk in Juba District Council. Tembura was certainly regarded as one of the leaders of the South, mainly for his role in the 'Juba Conference', as well as being one of the Southern clerk leaders.

Upon arrival of all members in Khartoum, the Legislative Assembly elected a president subject to the approval of the Governor-General and was of three categories: 65 elected; 10 appointed and the members of the Governor-General's Executive Council.

Among the 65 elected members ten (10) were elected directly by voters; 42 were elected indirectly by an electoral committee composing of members provincial councils; leading public figures, civil servants and representatives of towns and urban centers. Thirteen (13) representatives of the South were supposed to be elected by the provincial councils of Equatoria, Upper Nile, and Bahr El-Ghazal. Howver, due to the reasons discussed earlier this process was not executed by the law.

Among other things, the Assembly had no right to challenge the articles of the constitutional decree, nor was it allowed to pass laws on matters concerning foreign affairs, defense, currency, nationality and the status of the racial minorities and religion. The Assembly was mandated to last for three years. In present of the thirteen Southern representatives, an All-Sudan Legislative Assembly was officially inaugurated on 15 December 1948.[5]

The Evolution of the Southern Political Groups

As shall be discussed below, the awakening and the evolution of the Southern political consciousness went through difficult processes, sometimes, chaotic. In fact, many factors, social groups, and individuals contributed directly or indirectly in promoting this awareness. In general, the idea of 'South' as a political concept emerged in terms of opposition to the Muslim-Arab North. A Southerner before 1948 was primarily non-existed. Even if it was considered that such identity existed, it was based on tribal affiliation or career orientation i.e. a Shilluk clerk is a shilluk first and a government clerk second.

The British administrators in the South were however, instrumental, unintentionally perhaps, in creating a Southern political group embodied in the (13) Southern representatives in the Legislative Assembly. Individual Southerners found themselves involved in the Southern workers' Union; provincial councils in the South, which provided a satisfactory forum for political debates; underground organizations such as 'political committees' served as a political forums where Southern intellectuals meet.

Moreover, external pressures such as political developments in the North during the 1950's made it possible for Southerners to group themselves into a political force. Political and constitutional future of the south, especially in 1953, led to the formation of the first southern party. Therefore, the development of the above groups and their emergence into a Southern organized party and the activities of the Liberal party prior to and two years after the independence represented a shift in the north-south relations.

Workers' Union in the South
The advent of an organized Workers' Union in the three Southern provinces did not at its earlier stages have political objectives. Yet, these workers were conscious of their differences from Northern workers, despite their educational and occupational foundations. In 1950 for example, there were already three registered Workers' Unions in the South. These were the Government Elementary Masters Union; the intermediate Non-Government School teachers Union; and the Bahr El-Ghazal Saw Mill Workers' Union. In addition to these, there were other active unions such as Government Clerks Union, Hospital Warders Union, and many others. Most of these unions ere, however, poorly organized, hence did not play

any significant role, except in the realm of activities which directly affected their members. Thus, their main concern was wages and promotions of their members. Their members were virtually not allowed to involve in political discussions or membership to any organization that discusses political issues. This might explain why few information regarding the organizational structures and activities of these unions are not available.

The dominant examples of the southern Workers' Union early activities were the two strikes in Malakal in March 1943 and in Juba in October 1947. Although most of the union leaders denied any direct involvement in these strikes, their actions and participation in these strikes proved beyond doubt their intentions and responsibility in instigating these strikes. Furthermore, these strikes had shown the dissatisfaction of the Southern workers of the prevailing conditions.

The Malakal Strike
On March 25, 1943 at 6:00 A.M. The Southern staff at Malakal Hospital went on strike. The objective of the strike was an attempt to remind the government of its policy towards the southern Workers in general. They petitioned the Hospital administration asking why the workers in Malakal had not received the war allowances, which had been approved for their Northern counterparts. The senior medical officer in charge, Dr. Prattassued told them that the delay was not intentional, and assured them that their allowances would be approved retroactively to January 1st, 1943. Having received

assurances that the demands will be met, the workers returned to work. However, the Upper Nile government was angered by this unprecedented move and as such decided to punish the ringleaders of the strike. Their spokesmen were whipped publicly, but no further action was taken.[6]

However, according to some government officials in Malakal, the strike was not caused mainly by the war allowances, nor did the strike came as a surprise. It is reported that the British doctors at the hospital had consistently complained about unbalanced condition of the hospital where Southern and Northern officials working side by side doing the same job, but with a big discrepancies in pay. To the British political officers in the province, the effect of this unequal treatment on the morale of the Southern staff was deplorable.[7] In other words, frustrated by an inferiority complex, which seemed to have been endorsed by the government paying them less, it was no a surprise that Southern workers felt bitter sense of inequality. Thus, the Malakal strike seemed to have been a first warning to the government that something has to be done on the rate pay of the Southern workers.

The Juba Strike
On October 1st, 1947, the British officials in Juba town were unexpectedly surprised by a strike of workers both skilled and unskilled, who were joined on the next day by the clerical staff. Although the provincial government did not find evidence that it has agitated the strike, the newly formed 'Southern Sudan Welfare Committee (SSWC)', whose

membership composed of (240) Southern educated clerical workers, assumed the leadership of the strike. Among other concerns, their principal demands were better wages for themselves as well as for the unskilled hospital attendants, sanitary workers and laborers.[8]

According to the government account, on the first day of the strike, over hundred workers closed the road from the countryside to Juba town. Unlike the Malakal strike four years earlier, cars were stoned and public buildings were attacked. The government reacted by calling in a company of the Equatorial Corps from Torit District, since the police in Juba chose to sympathize with the strikers. Three days later, the acting governor, A.C. Beaton, met with strikers. The SSWC leaders presented a list composed of nineteen demands on top of, which was insufficient pay and the system of differentiated pay of scales for Northern and Southern Sudanese.

In order for strikers to return to their work, they asked the government to receive and acknowledge officially the list of their grievances. The government accepted this condition, and on October 5th, their complaints were presented to Beaton and the strike was lifted.[9]

Unlike the Malakal strike, the Juba strike soon spread to Wau, Yambio, Nzara and Tonj in Bahr al-Ghazal. In Wau town, the strike was led by the SSWC branch director Khamis Mursal, a storekeeper in the public works' department. Also in Wau, the hospital dressers' union had the most contact with Northerners, more active and formed the prominent element of the strike in Wau. The SSWC leaders in city departments, having received assurances that their demands will be met they asked the workers return to their works.

In Nzara and Yambio the situation was different. The District Commissioner, Mr. Tiger Wyld, reacted to the strike by dismissing a few and accepted force resignation of some other workers. At Tonj District, the strikers were more cohesive, due to the presence of Clement Mboro, whose presence maintained the strength of the strikers. At the time, Clement Mboro was emerging as one of the most able rising Southern intelligentsia. The strike under his leadership lasted for four days, October 9-13, after which Mr. Wyld accepted to receive the strikers' complaints.[10]

Although most of their demands were not met, the leaders of the Malakal and Juba strikes tried to make their dissatisfaction clear to the government. In fact, these strikes represented visible symbols of practical and personal nature of differences between Southern and Northern employment policies. Moreover, most of these workers represented at the time the 'Southern enlightened' leadership hence, the strikes symbolized the beginning of the Southern awareness as a political force responsible for the destiny of the Southern Sudan.

Clement Mboro recognized this fact when he said:

"... the strikes led to the recognition of the Southern intellectuals as a force to be reckoned with".[11]

Thus, the role of the workers' Union in the South, though limited, did play an important role in the emergence of the

Southern Sudanese consciousness, needless to mention that it was among these workers that Southern representatives to the 'Juba Conference' in 1947 were selected.

The Southern Sudan Welfare Committee (SSWC)
Little is known about the origins and structural organization of the Southern Sudan Welfare Committee, except that the government recognized it as a social welfare organization solely concerned with social aspects of Southern government's workers. Its activities were not to include political issues. It did not have an official newspaper through which its activities and programs could have reached its members. That is why little information available is found in the government files in form of petitions, provincial reports, arrest of its members, punishment of its leaders etc.

The Southern Sudan Welfare Committee (SSWC) was founded in November 1946 in Juba town. Its first president was Stanislaus Paysama, few months later, the committee established branches in Malakal, Wau and in a few other Southern towns. The committee was formed to be 'a social society' composing of clerks and bookkeepers. However, it was not long when it acquired a political role; its leaders were nominated to go to 'Juba Conference' and later on assumed an active role in promoting the Southern cause.

The committee did not have an organized structure and had no regular meetings, laws or constitution. Although none of its members accepted this assertion, the nature of the meetings of its members seems to support this statement. Its members met in clubs, houses or in their offices and talked.[12] The committee in a way represented the aims and views of all Southern staff, particularly the lower grades or the category of 'Article II' as it was called.

It is to be recalled that on Friday June 13, 1947 after the close of the formal 'Juba Conference' sessions, Sir James Robertson convened a meeting of sub-committee to the 'Juba Conference' at the Province headquarters. A group of Southern Sudan Welfare Committee leaders was selected to attend the meeting for the purpose of hearing their grievances over wages.13 Before the SSWC was established the civil and financial secretaries were solely dependent on the three southern governors to represent the interests of their employees. Prior to the subcommittee meeting, there was no governor ready to pressurize for change of wages of the southern workers, who were small, unorganized and unhappy. The meeting was attended by five government representatives: James Robertson, F. D. Kingdon, B. V. Marwood, G. H. Barter, and T. R. Jolan. The SSWC was represented by Clement Mboro, Edward Dedigo, James Tembura, Siricio Iro and Hassan Fertak. The Northern Sudanese were represented by Dr. Habib Abdulla and Hassan Affendi Ahamed Osman.[14] The meeting discussed all the conditions facing Southern staff in all their aspects. The Civil Secretary promised the SSWC leaders that the decisions of the meeting will be taken upon his return to Khartoum. The significant of the meeting seemed to lay on the fact that SSWC, for the first time, was recognized as the sole representative of the southern workers.

Provincial Councils

Soon after the 'Juba Conference' of June 1947, Sir James Robertson asked the three Southern governors to start the formation of the provincial councils. These councils were political forums in which issues related to Southern political status would be discussed. Therefore, the provincial councils, in theory, stood for mini-assemblies in the South where Southern intellectuals would learn the art of politics. They were also responsible for supervision of (13) Southern representatives in the Legislative Assembly.

The first council was established in Juba in May 1948 and in November councils were created in Upper Nile and Bahr El-Ghazal. The members of these councils were to select the southern members to the Legislative Assembly. Representatives of the three Southern provinces were to meet annually in the dry season. The 'Provincial Secretariat' was responsible for the preparation of the venue and the agenda of the meetings. The provincial councils' meetings were attended by the thirteen Southern representatives in the Legislative Assembly. During these meetings they were during these discussions subjected to sharp criticism.[15]

Among the main topics of the discussions were education, urban growth and scale of wages. Social problems such as prisoners, medical care, increasing consumption of Alcohol and taxes dominated the discussions. Although these councils were meant to promote political awareness among Southern intelligentsia, the pace of their activities was slow to achieve that goal. This was probably because the participants knew little about politics and seemed not interested to learn.[16]

Political Committees

The 'Political Committees' was a name given to the social gatherings of the Southerners in the Southern administrative towns. These 'committees' were dominated by informal discussions among Southern intellectuals in clubs, bars and in offices. There was no proper organization nor was there formal agendas. These discussions centered around follow up of events in the South through rumor and gossip. Over beer in the evenings, the 'committees' members discussed everything that they heard of, real or imaginary. The activities of these 'committees' varied from town to another and dependent on the political maturity of leadership of each committee. The most active committee was that of Juba under Paul Logali.[17]

In an attempt to transform these committees into 'political parties,' many provincial committees changed their names. In Equatoria for example a 'Southern United Party' was formed; later on changed its name to 'Southern Political Association' and 'Southern Sudan Social and Political Association'. In Upper Nile Both Diu formed 'Upper Nile Political Association'. In Khartoum Michael Watta took an initiative in forming "the Southern Sudan Federal Party". All these attempts aimed at organizing a united Southern party, which would safeguard the Southern interests in the Legislative Assembly. This was necessitated by inability of the (13) representatives to influence politically the decisions of the Assembly.[18]

On March 26, 1951 a constitutional Amendment Commission was appointed to recommend to the Governor-General some necessary recommendations. A British Judge, Mr. Stanley Baker, headed the Commission; Both Diu represented the South. The later demanded a special status in the Sudan; his demands were rejected on the ground that they were not realistic and dangerous for the national unity. Both Diu later withdrew from the Commission on the ground that:

> *"The Northern members proved to be intransigent in not accepting either of my two proposals: separation or unity with constitutional guarantees for the South."*[19]

Thus, the creation of the constitutional commission in March 1951 was the first event that stimulated Southerners to think of forming a political party.[20] Pointing out the consequences of Southern withdrawal from the commission, the British members on the commission managed to include 'safeguards' embodied in article (100) of the proposed 'self-government statute'. This article aimed at providing the South with a status similar to that of Northern Ireland in the United Kingdom.[21] The draft was based on the ground that:

> *"... the Governor-General shall have executive and administrative powers in the South".*[22]

The Northern members of the Legislative Assembly passed this draft with the intention of defeating it outside the Assembly. As the draft was forwarded to the Condominium authorities for approval in November 1952, the Northern politicians went back and forth to Cairo and succeeded in removing the safeguards granted to the South in the original draft to be replaced by the following provision:

> *"The Governor-General shall have a special respon-*
> *sibility to ensure fair equitable treatment of* all
> *inhabitants of* various provinces *of the Sudan."*

Outside Sudan, other important developments took place, which had affected the political future of the Sudan. On October 8, 1951, the Egyptian Wafd Government unilaterally abrogated the Anglo-Egyptian Agreement of 1936 and terminated the Anglo-Egyptian Agreement of January 1899, which created the Condominium over Sudan.[23]

A year later King Farouk was dethroned from his throne in July 23, by a military coup, which brought to power General Mohamed Naguib. Himself a half Sudanese, General Naguib tried to resolve rapidly the previous conflicts and confusion. The new leadership had shown willingness to approve the self-determination for Sudan.[24]

The second event that led to the unification of Southern intellectuals into a united front was what later became known as 'Jambo Affair'. It was reported that on December 28, 1952, Major Salah Salim, the Egyptian Minister in charge of the Sudanese affairs, arrived in Juba. On his arrival he refused to

81

meet the official delegation waiting to receive him. Instead, the Major appeared at night, unannounced, in Amadi district on December 31st. The man with whom he was acquainted disappeared and was seen no more in Juba. This is how the 'Jambo Affair' began.[25]

Little is known about Jambo Lowoh, except that he was chief of the Beriba clan of the Moru tribe. He was succeeded to the chieftainship in 1929, having terminated his service in police force. He was ambitious man and eventually gained the position of the Amadi (B) court.

The story goes as follows: on the night of December 29, 1952, Jambo Lowoh and a certain chief Wajo signed a document presented to the Major Salim entitled "proposals and demands for Southern Sudan". In this document the two chiefs submitted that, "the South agreed to the policy of support for Egypt and the Northern Sudanese".[26] The document condemned and accused the British officials of sowing seeds of enmity among the people of Moru. The Major tried to persuade other chiefs to sign the document but they refused. On the same night Major Salim left for Juba; demonstrations broke out the next day in Amadi demanding Jambo's dismissal; he was eventually removed from his post as a president of Amadi court. The chief remained a controversial figure in the Southern Sudanese politics. Later on, he was seen returning from Cairo with "smart new tarbush".[27] Many questions remained unanswered" What was the connection between the Major Salim and chief Jambo? How and when did they forge their contact? What power did chief Jambo possess to represent the Southern political opinion? He seemed to have felt that his main rival, chief Timon Biro, was succeeding in ousting him as president of the Amadi court, and hence tried to maintain his power. When the Southern leaders heard about this affair, especially the members of the Legislative Assembly, thy decided to form the 'Southern Party'.

Anglo-Egyptian Agreement of February 12, 1953

The third event that stimulated or rather accelerated the formation of the Southern party was their reaction to the February 12, 1953 Anglo-Egyptian Agreement. That Agreement laid the foundation for liquidation of the Condominium and was the first step toward self-determination.[28] During the negotiations and signing of this agreement Southerners excluded.

It is to be recalled that on October 30, 1952 pro-independence Northern Sudanese parties and the Egyptian government signed a separate Agreement calling for administrative autonomy in the Sudan by the end of 1953. It was on the basis of the Egyptian proposal of November 2, 1952 that an Agreement was signed between Great Britain and Egypt on 12 February 1953 which "called upon the Sudanese to exercise their right to self-determination within a period of three years".[29]

On the other hand, the pro-Egyptian leaders in the North remained committed to their position that Egypt had unilaterally abrogated the 1899 Condominium Agreement and the 1936 Treaty f alliance; and hence they did not sign the Agreement.

In the Northern point of view, two reasons were behind the exclusion of the Southern Sudanese in the Anglo-Egyptian negotiations of 1952 which led eventually to the February 1953 Agreement:

The South had no political parties to send to Cairo in order to attend the negotiations.

The Northern Sudanese argued that the 'unity' between the North and the South was achieved in 1947, so it was legitimate for the Northern politicians to represent the Sudanese as people and the Sudan as one political unit.[30]

Concerning the Southern Sudan, Article 5 of the Anglo-Egyptian Agreement of February 12, 1953 read as follows:

> *"The two contracting governments agreed that it being a fundamental principle of their common policy to maintain the unity of the Sudan as a single territory (South and North), the special powers which are vested on the Governor-General by Article 100 of the self-government statute shall not be exercise in any manner which is in conflict with that policy."*[31]

Southern reaction to the government was that of indifference, frustration and anger. Almost all the Southern politicians lost the little faith they had in British officials. Instead they began to rely on themselves by using direct methods for the attainment of their goals, than reliance on the government. As a first step of its kind, Both Biu, the Secretary General of the newly formed 'South Party', protested against the Agreement to the United Nations Organization.[32] This action was considered by the northerners as an attempt from Southern side to internationalize the 'Southern problem'.

Another Southern reaction came on December 13, 1952, in form of memorandum by the president of the 'Juba Political Committee' Paul Logali, addressed to the government. While reiterating the support of the Southerners to the self-Government statute as approved by the Legislative Assembly, the memorandum rejected any modification to that statute. Logali memorandum went on to say:

> "The people of the southern Sudan have raised the present political issues because leaders of the political parties in the Northern Sudan after coming to and agreement with the South in 1947, the logical culmination of which was expressed in the self-government statute, made unilateral agreement with General Naguib without consultation with the South. This made the people of the South doubt the good faith of the Northern political leaders."[33]

Based on the discussion above, it seemed that the emerging Southern political community was sidelined and ignored in consultations that were taking place on the future of the country. In other words, the reaction of the leaders of Southern Sudan to the 1953 agreement appeared to have adopted a 'wait and see attitude'.

In Yei Town, for example, the Southerners showed a greater interest in the free beer at a certain Ali's coffee shop than the

District Commissioner's announcement of the treaty. In Juba, all the Bari chiefs boycotted a celebration feast by the Northern merchants, marking the new Agreement. In Malakal and Wau, sit-in strikes at various government departments too place.

The Southern Liberal Party

The first attempt to establish an organized political organization, which included Southern Sudanese, was in 1949, when the short-lived 'Black Bloc' was formed. The founder of this group was Dr. Adam Adham, a Western Sudanese member of Legislative Assembly. This group composed of the Nuba, Fur and Southern Sudanese. The Bloc was concerned with political equality of the Blacks of the Sudan. In the South, the organization was received by the same indifference with which the people of the South regarded the Legislative Assembly in Khartoum.[34] i.e. fear and suspicion. The Bloc was considered by some southern Sudanese as 'a new face' of 'Northern Sudanese' and a plot, which aimed at assimilating the Southern Sudan into Northern political domination.[35]

The 'Black Bloc' did not survive long; political differences among its members led to its disintegration. The appointment of the first Southern group to the Legislative Assembly introduced these members into new political realities. In fact, the influence of Northern political parties, Umma Party and the National Unionist party (NUP), encouraged the thirteen Southerners to launch a political movement in the South. Thus, thanks to the development of the Workers' Union, provincial councils, 'political committees' and the Legislative Assembly,

political awareness crystallized into distinct political movement in the South.

The 'Southern Sudanese Political Movement' was established in 1951. The birth of the movement was pioneered by
three leaders: Stanslaus Paysama, its President, Both Diu, its
Secretary General and Abdel Rahman Sule its Patron.[36] In 1952,
the movement changed its name to the 'Southern Party'. The
party remained inactive until disappointed at their non-rep-
resentation on national political issues, and determined that
their voices should be heard in the future, that many Southern
intellectuals decided joined the party.

For the Southern party to participate in the general election
as stipulated in the Anglo-Egyptian Agreement of 1953, the
party was registered officially in 1953. According to Siricio
Iro, an active member of the party, the Southern party had to
change its name again later on in 1954, "to 'Liberal party' to
avoid strong geographical and location identification, reflected
in the former name.[37] The change of the name was an attempt
from the Liberal Party to attract members from other parts
of the country, especially among Western and Eastern Sudan
politicians to join their party. However, it turned out to be
unsuccessful gesture, and the party was forced to change its
name again, this time to the 'Southern Liberal Party'.

Therefore, the party had used three different names since
its inception in 1951, Southern political movement, Southern
party, and Liberal party, before adopting the name 'Southern
Liberal Party'.[38] The leadership and organizational structure
of the Southern Liberal Party was formed as follows in 1953:

Benjamin Lwoki, Chairman

Stanslaus Paysama, Vice Chairman

Both Diu, Secretary General

Abdel Rahman Sule, Patron

The main objective of the party was to secure a self-government status for the South in form of a federation.[39] Immediately after reorganization, many Southern intellectuals were obliged to support the party on the understanding that this was the only legitimate organized Southern forum through which the South would be able to campaign in the forthcoming elections.

 From political perspective, the Southern Liberal Party played an important role in two crucial periods. The first two years which preceded independence, especially in connection with the 'Sudanization' of the government posts and the Southern share. Then, the two years that followed the independence before the military coup of November 1958.

As mentioned earlier, in accordance with the provisions of Article (7) of the Anglo-Egyptian Agreement of 1953 concerning the self-government and self-determination of the Sudan, an Electoral Commission was to be established. Article (7) reads as follows:

"There shall be constituted an mixed Electoral Commission of seven Members. There shall be three Sudanese appointed by the Governor- General with approval of his commission, one Egyptian citizen, one citizen of United Kingdom, one citizen of United

> *States of America, and one Indian... The Indian*
> *member shall be chairman of the commission.*"[40]

The Electoral Commission was formally appointed on the
April 8th, 1953 as follows:
Sumuk-Amar, Indian, Chairman
Abdel Fattah Hassan, Egypt
J. C. Penney, United Kingdom
Warwick Perkins, United States of America
Abdel Salam El-Khalifa, Northern Sudanese
Khalafalla Khalid, Northern Sudanese
Gordon Bulli, Southern Sudanese [41]

According to Article (31) of the self-Government Statute,
the share of Southern Sudan in the Senate was as follows:

Bahr El-Ghazal Province	3 seats
Equatoria Province	2 seats
Upper Nile Province	3 seats
Total	8 seats

According to the Senate electoral procedure members were to
be elected indirectly by provincial courts, voting as a single
Electoral College.[42] In addition, the South was also allocated
(3) seats of the graduates.[43]

On the other hand, Article (32) of the Statute allocated
twenty-two (22) constituencies of the House of Representatives
to the three Southern provinces as follows:

Bahr El-Ghazal Province	7 seats
Equatoria Province	7 seats
Upper Nile Province	8 seats
Total	22 seats

During the November-December campaign for the first Sudanese parliamentary elections, each of the main Northern political parties, Umma and the National Unionist party, the later backed by Egypt, tried to win the Southern votes. The Egyptian Minister, Major Salah Salim, visited the South in November 1953, where he campaigned on behalf of the NUP. At one point he promised Southerners (40) senior posts in the government. In Wau, where he joined a Dinka dance, hence got the name of "Dancing Officer", the Major tried to convince his co-dancers by blaming the heat of the sun for the differences in color between him and Southern Sudanese.[44]

For the description of the seats allocated to the three Southern provinces refer to tables 2, 3 and 4 below:

Table 2

Seats Allocated to the Bahr- Al Ghazal Province in the House of Representative in 1953 Elections.

Name of Constituency	Description
1. Western Bahr al-Ghazal	Western District, Bahr El-Ghazal
2. Aweil East	Poliet and Abiyam
3. Aweil West	Palioping and Malwal
4. Jur River North	Gogrial Northern part of Jur River District
5. Jur River South	Rest of Jur River District
6. Rumbek	Western part of Lakes District
7. Yirol	Eastern part of lakes District

Total of seats = 7

Source: Documents on the Sudan, 189901953, (Egyptian Society of International Law, March 1953), p. 94.

Table 3

Allocated to the Equatoria Province in the House of
Representative in 1953 Elections

Name of Constituency	Description
1. Eastern Equatoria	Eastern District of Equatoria
2. Torit	Torit District
3. Yei	Yei District
4. Juba	Juba District
5. Moru	Moru District
6. Zande East	Yambio and Ibba Sub-District
7. Zande West	Ezo Sub-District

Total of Seats = 7

Source: Documents on the Sudan, 1899-1953, (Egyptian Society of International Law, March 1953), p. 94.

Table 4

Seats Allocated to the Upper Nile Province in the House of
Representative in 1953 Elections

Name of Constituency	*Description*
Western Nuer Ghazal	Western Nuer District of Bahr El-Ghazal
Western Nuer Jebel	Western Nuer Dist lying between Bahr Al- Ghazal and Bahr Al-Jabel
Central Nuer East	Lou Nuer and Central Nuer District Dinka
Zeraf Valley	Zeraf Island and Gaweir Nuer
Pibor and Eastern Nuer	Pibor and Eastern Nuer District
Bor	Bor District
Shiluk	Shiluk Adminstration
Renk and Malakal	Renk and Malakal Districts

Total of Seats = 8

Source: Documents on the Sudan, 1899-1953, (Egyptian Society of International Law, March 1953), p. 95.

However, several factors hindered the Southern Liberal Party overall victory in the South. Among these were:

- The illiteracy of the voters
- Lack of proper lists of the names of voters
- The long distances the voters had to walk in order to cast their votes
- The age set for voters and candidates were twenty-one and thirty years consecutively.[45]

On the other hand, almost all Southerners at the time did not have birth certificates; thus, many Liberal Party supporters lost their constitutional right to vote or to be elected. They were either considered underage or their names did not appear on the tax lists used for polling in the Southern electoral stations. The Northern army and the (NUP) partisans in the South used all kinds of intimidation tricks and blackmailing, which terrified the Liberal candidates and forced some of them to withdraw their candidacy. Some of Southern government employees were bribed to refrain from working as agents of the Liberal Party.

The Egyptian Irrigation Departments in Malakal and Juba towns led the press election campaign by distributing pamphlets, and sometimes bribes those who were working against the Southern-NUP candidates.[46] It is to be noted that at its early stages, the Southern Liberal Party did not constitute a well-organized group as was the other Northern political parties. However, there was no Liberal Party member who could risk appearing opponent of 'federalism', the main objective of the party; although some Southerners were won over to the NUP party, most probably for financial needs.

When the NUP won the elections, the Southern Liberal
Party allied with the Umma Party in an official opposition.
This alliance came as a result of conviction that both parties
opposed the unity of the Sudan with Egypt and both were for
total independence of the Sudan; hence they were supporting
the British presence in the country till independence. Despite
Major Salah Salim's efforts, the NUP won only six out of the
twenty-two Southern seats, which were won by independent
candidates.[47] On January 6th, 1954 the victorious NUP leader,
Ismail al-Azhari, was elected the first Sudan Prime Minister,
naming an all-NUP cabinet. According to the self-Government
statute, two Southerners should be cabinet members; instead,
Al-Azhari named three, all of whom were NUP members. The
three were not given portfolios; they were Bullen Alier, Santino
Deng, and Dak Deth, a member from central Nuer East.[48]

The Sudanization
The Sudanese parliament met officially on January 1st, 1954.
The Prime Minister's first assignment was, as stipulated in the
Anglo-Egyptian Agreement of February 1953, the appointment
of 'a Sudanization Committee'. This public service commis-
sion was appointed on February 20th, 1954, and composed
mostly of Northern Sudanese. Al-Azhari named:
  Ibrahim Yusuf Sulayman, Northern Sudanese
  Dr. Uthman Abu Akar , Northern Sudanese
  Muhammed al-Fudli. Egypt
  Abd al-Hamid Daud, Egypt
  R. B. Burnett, Britain

The work of the Sudanization Committee was to recommend plans for Sudanization of administration, which included Sudan defense Force, police and other government posts that may affect the freedom of the Sudanese at the time of self-determination. It is to be recalled that the National Unionist party had already promised Southerners during its election campaign in the South that:

> "Not only shall priority be always given to the Southerners in the South but also the employment of Southerners shall greatly fostered in the North, especially in higher ranks of central government service; the District Commissioners, Governors, Deputy Governors and in general they will have greater of jobs in the Sudan."[49]

In the South, the results of the Sudanization committee were anxiously awaited at the very time that the relations between the North and the South were rapidly deteriorating. At a rally of the Southern Liberal Party held at Malakal on August 27th, 1954, attended by over three hundred supporters, the principal speakers, Abdel Rahman Sule and Both Diu, stressed the "promotion of Southerners for higher posts in the administration and police".[50]

For the distributions of Sudan defense Force, police and other government posts refer to table 5.

Table 5

Classified British Posts to be Sudanized

Agriculture Dept.	156
Education Dept.	141
Public works Dept.	162
Railways Dept.	42
Irrigation Dept.	48
Finance Dept.	21
Post and Telegraphs Dept.	44
Mechanical Transport Dept.	40
Veterinary Service	35
Provincial Administration	116
Ministry of Interior	13
Police	6
Total	1,156

The results of the Sudanization Committee for those to be appointed to senior posts in the South were announced in October 1954. The outcome came as a shock to the Southern Liberal Party as well as to the Southern-NUP members. This disappointment was expressed by Gregoria Deng Kir, a Southern trader in Gogrial district who summed up the prevailing situation in the South in the following words:

> *"The results of the Sudanization have come with a very disappointing results: i.e. four District Commissioners and two ma'murs; well as it appears,*

it means our fellow Northerners want to colonize us
for another hundred years."[51]

Thus, out of 800 posts, the South was allotted only 6 admin-istrative posts. In general terms, the Sudanization results brought more friction with the Southern-NUP members on the one hand, and between them and the Prime Minister. In reaction to the Sudanization outcome, two NUP Southern cabinet members, Bullen Alier and Dak Deth, resigned from al-Azhari government.

Meanwhile, on 25 September 1954, the NUP-Southern members of parliament met in Juba, the attendants were; Bullen Alier, Dak Deth, John Majok, Phelimon Majok, Akech Rizgallah, Michah Belkikan, Niduha Akech, Abdel Nabi Abdel Gadir Murssal, Gordon Ayom, Ridso Onzi, and Cosmos Rababa. In memorandum to the Prime minister, the parliamentarians warned the government of a great trouble in the South and stressed that unless the demands of the South are met, there would be no other alternative to solve the 'Southern Problem', except more chaos. Their memo was accompanied by a list of what they called 'General Outlay of Demands of Posts' to which Southerners should be appointed. (See Table 6).

Table 6

General Outlay of Demands of Posts presented to the Prime Minister, Ismail Al-Azhari, by the NUP-Southern Members on 25 September 1954

Administrative Positions

Position	Numbers
Governors	3
Deputy Governors	3
District Commissioners	6
Assistant District Commissioners	8
Mamurs	12
Assistant Mamurs	Open
Prison Officers	3
Other Positions (Prison)	Open
Police Commandant	4
Police Officers	3
Other Positions (Police)	Open

Position	Numbers
Scale F	4
Scale DS	6
Scale J	12
Scale H	Open

Accountants

Position	Numbers
Scale F	4
Scale DS	6
Scale J	12
Scale H	Open

Forestry

Position	Numbers
Scale F	4
Scale DS	6
Scale J	12
Scale H	Open

Position	Numbers
Scale F	4
Scale J	6
Scale H	12
Scale KJH	Open

Agriculture

Position	Numbers
Scale J	5
Scale H	12

Medical Assistants

Position	Numbers
Scale F	3
Scale J	3
Scale H	6

Medical Laboratories

Position	Numbers
Scale J	5
Scale H	5
Scale B	Open

Health

Position	Numbers
Scale DS	2
Scale F	3
Scale J	12

Local Government Salaries

Position	Salary
District Court	£20
Salary of Zu'ama	£10
Salary of Assistant Zu'ama	£5
Salary of Provincial Councilors	£2.5
Salary of Court Clerks	£6-10
Salary of Shiluk King (reth)	£80

Source: Report of Commission of inquiry into Disturbances in Southern Sudan, 1955, pp. 136-7.

On the other hand, in October 1954, the Southern Liberal Party convened a meeting at Juba Dance Hall. The subject of discussion was the results of the Sudanization committee. Most of the speakers expressed their views variably, but with one them,

Joshua Malwal demanded secession, if administration was not 'Southernned'; chief Fahal Ukanda demanded Federation for the South; Andrea Farajalla suggested full independence for the people of the South. On October 21, 1954, a resolution calling 'Federal status' for the South was passed, and the conferees called upon the Southerners to be ready for sacrifices.[52]

It worth mentioning that few at that meeting conceptualized that they were to be called later on to make sacrifices, and perhaps some of those present imagined the magnitude of the 'Southern Sudan problem'. However, as the Liberals left the meeting hall on October 21st 1954, some of them at least seemed to have noticed the difficulties they were going to face since their guardians, the British, were leaving.[53]

By and large, the exclusion of Southerners from the senior administration posts left a great resentment among the Liberal Party leaders. Having learned from the Sudanization results that the South was to be governed by Northerners, most of whom had little experience of the region, the educated Southerners, government officials and especially the Liberal Party members, made it a point to frustrate work of the new administrators in the South.

Secondly, the Southern politicians, for the first time, grouped themselves and supported the Liberal Party against the government that had accepted the Sudanization results.54 Hence the year 1954 marked the first wave of the Southern Liberal Party mobilization throughout the South. The second wave of the Liberal Party's mobilization across the Southern Sudan came in May 1955 when the Southern-NUP members of parliament joined officially the Southern Liberal Party. The new comers and the Liberals in the parliament formed a 'Southern Parliamentary Bloc'. The Bloc called for a conference in Juba in which a constitution embodying the 'federal status' would be discussed. Despite the Prime Minister's attempts to frustrate it, the conference was convened on 5-6 July 1955 and passed important resolution among which were the following:

- Unity among Southerners
- The guarantee of special status for the Southern Sudan within United Sudan
- The demand for a federal state

The conference selected a ten-man delegation, led by Both Diu, to go to Khartoum with recommendations of the conference to be distributed to the Northern parties. The task of the delegation was to negotiate the demand of the federal status for the South before the declaration of independence in January 1955.[55]

However, before the delegation receive official respond from the Prime Minister, 'disturbances' broke out in August 1955 throughout the South; these 'disturbances' culminated into mutiny of Southern corps in Torit town on 18 August 1955. The mutiny became the nuclei of the 'Anyanya' gurrella movement in the South, which fought the first civil war in the region (1955-1972). The army was flown in from the North; peace was eventually restored, but tension remained high.[56]

The Liberal Party leadership was implicated to have been the main instigator of the mutiny. Certain documents were produced which carried the names of some liberal politicians, but these documents did not bear their partnership to the mutiny. The causes and the full account of the mutiny shall be discussed in a separate chapter.

Following the mutiny, state of emergency was declared in the South, thus all political activities of the Liberal Party were confined in the North. On 19th December 1955, the parliament met to consider endorsement of a motion for independence proposed by the Northern parties. As a condition for their support to the Northern motion, the Southern Bloc proposed a federal system to be established in the country. In fact, the Southern leadership only supported the Northern plan for an independent Sudan with clear understanding that a federalism granting equality to Christianity and English with Islam and Arabic would be seriously considered by the Constitutional Committee. They further stated that if their proposal is not taken into consideration, a plebiscite was to be held in the South under the auspices of the United Nations or the International Red Cross.

As a compromise, the Northern parties accepted to insert the following loose provision in the motion of the independence:

> "The request by the Southern members of parliament for a federal status for the South will be given full consideration by the Constituent Assembly."[57]

With this provision inserted, the Liberal Party along with Northern parties passed the motion for independence unanimously.

On the 1st January 1956, the self-Government statute ceased to operate and the transition constitution came into force. The Republic of the Sudan became independent state on that day. It is to be recalled that on 8 September 1955, and in accordance with the Commission of Inquiry Ordinance of 1954, a commission was appointed to, "inquire into and to report on the recent disturbances in the Southern Sudan and their underlying causes".[58] The commission was chaired by Taufiq Cotran, a Palestinian police magistrate in Khartoum. The membership of the commission composed of Khalifa Magoub a Northern Sudanese and chief Lado Lolik a Southerner. The commission submitted its report to the Interior Minister, Ali Abdel Rahman, on 18th February 1956. It was published in October 1956. The report is widely regarded as the best, fair and neutral document prepared till then on the problem of Southern Sudan.

A new coalition was formed on 7th July 1956 between Umma, People's Democratic Party (PDP) and the Southern Liberal Party. The new Prime Minister was Abdulla Bey Khalil of the Umma party. On 30th June 1957, the parliament was dissolved in preparation for elections, which took place from 27 February to 9 March 1958. As a result, two hundred and three (203) legislators were elected: 173 representatives (Umma 63; NUP 45; PDP 27; the newly formed Federal Party 40 and 30 Senators. Fr. Saturnino Lohure became the leader of the Southern Parliamentary Bloc. The main task of the new Constituent Assembly was the making of a permanent constitution for the country. The question was whether the Sudan was to be parliamentary or presidential (refer to table 7).[59]

Table 7

Name of the Party	1953	1958	1965	1967	1968
Federal Party	NE	40	NE	-	NE
Southern Liberal Party	16	-	NE	1	NE
SANU (Inside)	NE	NE	-	10	15
Southern Front	NE	NE	-	-	10
Independents	-	11	-	3	-

NE = None Exist.

Source: Woodward, Peter, "Is Sudan Governable: Some Thoughts on the Experience of Liberal Democracy and Military Rule", British Society for Middle Eastern Studies Bulletin 2 (1987), pp. 137-49

However, before the constitution was made, a new government elected by the members of the Assembly had to be formed. Three prominent politicians, including the former leader of the Southern Liberal Party, stood for the position of the Prime Minister with the following results:[60]

Name	Party	Votes	Observations
Abdalla Bey Kalil	Umma Party	103	Absent: Ezboni Mundiri
Ismail Al Azhari	National Unionist Party	44	
Stanslaus A. Paysama	Southern Parliament Bloc	25	

On April 21st, 1965 elections were held throughout Sudan, SANU faction William Deng and Southern Front boycotted elections. Northern merchants were declared unopposed MPs in the South and fifteen Umma-NUP Southerners were also seated in parliament in November 1965.

The Southern Bloc and the NUP formed an official opposition to the Umma-PDP coalition government. Earlier, in September 1957, a 47-member constitution committee, with membership of three Southerners, Fr. Saturnino Lohure representing the missions; Stanislaus Abdullah Paysama and Bullen Alier, was formed. The Southern members of the commission emphasized their demand for federal status, which should become part of the constitution. Their demand was rejected and the Northerners gave their final position stating that:

"the Southern claim for federation was given consideration and it was found out that it could not work in this country".[61]

The 3 Southern members of the commission withdrew leaving the 43 Northerners to go ahead drafting Unitary-Islamic Constitution. In May 1958 the draft was tabled before the Constituent Assembly for approval. On 16th June 1958 the Federal Party members of Parliament went to the House only to explain their view on the proposed draft of the constitution (the formation, objectives and activities of the southern Federal Party will be discussed in the next chapter). The leader of the Parliamentary Bloc, Fr. Saturnino Lohure, addressed the house as follows:

"Mr. President Sir, the South has no ill-intentions whatsoever toward the North; the South simply claims to run its local affairs in a United Sudan. The South has no intention of separating from the North, for had that been the case nothing on the earth would have prevented the demand for separation. The South claims to Federate with the North, a right that the South undoubtedly possess as a consequence of the principle of free self-determination which reason and democracy grant to free people. The South will at any moment separate from the North if and when the North so desires, directly or indirectly, through political, social and economic subjection of the South."[62]

It is to be pointed out that Joseph Oduho and Oliver Albino argued that most of 40 Southern parliamentarians who return from the South in February 1958 elections were either Liberal members or its sympathizers. However, Dustan Wai maintains that the Liberals lost all their seats to the young Federalists. However, Wai does not mention the name federalists, but he refers to young leadership.

Given the deadlock in the parliament, and democracy being practiced, the parliament could not go ahead with its deliberations. The Southern MPs said their word and left the House. Confused of not knowing what to do next, the Umma Party, the main partner in the coalition, struck a secret deal with the army and handed over the power to the military, led by

General Ibrahim Abboud on 17 November 1958. With Abboud, the parliamentary life came to an end only after two years of independence.63 With Aboud in power, all political parties in the country, top on the list the Federal Party, were dissolved.

Looking back to1947, it seems that the emergence of an organized Southern political consciousness had undergone difficult processes. The Liberals had continuously claimed what their colleagues demanded in 1947, a special status for the South. They tried to achieve it, but the mistrust between the South and the North continued to be an obstacle throughout. From labour leaders of Workers' Union, to provincial councils, political committees leaders, and legislative assembly members, the Liberal Party leaders had lived all the crucial stages of North-South relations. By 1958, they were ready to hand over the struggle to the young leaders, who called themselves, the "federalists". Throughout its life-time the Liberal Party employed different political tactics either by making alliances and maintaining contacts with Northern parties or by grouping themselves with other groups in the country, the Western and the Eastern Sudan parliamentarians.

However, like any political organization, the Liberal Party had its own weaknesses. Its members were divided, not on ethnic lines at the time, due of personal clashes over leadership. In fact, many southerners joined Northern political parties, not necessarily in opposition to the Liberal Party objectives rather some of them believed that by doing so, they would pursue Southern interests successfully within the dominant Northern establishment. It seems however that they were neither listened to, nor or respected; instead they were considered 'doves' susceptible to manipulation.

In 1957, Benjamin Lwoki, President of the Liberal Party, broke away with a small faction and joined PDP, while the other faction remained loyal to Stanslaus Paysama. In June 1957, Fr. Saturnino Lohure and Luigi Adwok voted in support of the government motion calling for acceptance of the US Aid, as a result they were both dismissed from the party positions by their colleagues.64 The two leaders were replaced by Elijah Mayom and Franco Garang as President and Secretary General of the Liberal Party respectively.

End Notes

1. Collins, *Shadows in the Grass*, pp. 412-3. These safeguards were previously raised in the 'Juba Conference', but the topic was referred to the Governor-General's executive council for study.

2. Daly, *Imperial Sudan*, pp. 241-2.

3. Sam C. Sarkensian. "The Southern Sudan: A Reassessment" *African Studies Review* 16 (1973), pp. 1-22.

4. Collins, *Shadows in the Grass*, pp. 432-35.

5. Ibid., p. 436.

6. Documents on the Sudan, 1899-1953, Egyptian Society of International Law, March 1953, pp. 34-41; Woodward, "Constitutional Development and Independence in the Sudan", pp. 114-120.

7. Collins, *Shadows in the Grass*, p. 442.

8. Ibid., p. 418; I prefer to use the name Workers' Union' rather than Trade Unions, for the later connotes modernity and sophistication.

9. K.D.D.Henderson, *Sudan Republic*, (London: Ernest Benn Limited, 1965) pp. 195-7.

10. Collins, *Shadows in the Grass*, pp. 425-7; Garretson, "The Southern Sudan Welfare Committee and the 1947 Strike in the Southern Sudan" *North East African Studies* 8, 2-3 (1986), pp. 181-91.

11. Collins., p. 426; Garretson, "The Southern Sudan Welfare Committee and the 1947 Strike...", pp. 181-91.

12. Collins., pp. 426.

13. Mohammed O. Bashir, *Tarih al –Harakh al Wataniya Fi al Sudan, 1899-1969* (Dar Al-Sudaniya Lil Kutub, 1980), pp. 248-51.

14. Collins, *Shadow in the Grass*, p. 422 ; Garretson, "The Southern Sudan Wefare Committee and the 1947 Strike ...", pp. 181-91.

15. Collins., p. 423.

16. Daly, *Imperial Sudan*, p. 261.; Garretson, "The Southern Sudan Welfare Committee and ...", pp. 181-91.

17. Collins, *Shadows in the Grass*, p. 439.

18. Ibid., pp. 442-43.

19. Henderson, *The Sudan Republic*, pp. 201-201.

20. Collins, *Shadows in the Grass*, P. 449.

21. Samson S. Wassara and Abdel Magid A. Bob, "The Emergence of Organized Political Movement in Southern Sudan 1946-1972" in *The Nationalist Movement in the Sudan,* edited by Mahasin Abdel Gadir Haj a-Safi,(Khartoum: University of Khartoum, 1989), pp. 295-321; Collins, *Shadows in the Grass,* p. 438.

22. Beshir, *Southern Sudan: Background to Conflict,* p. 7.

23. Farouk Akasha Abdun, *Education and Integration in the Sudan:A Historical Review* (Unpublished M. A. Thesis: Beirut, American University of Beirut, 1987), pp. 16-26.

24. Wassara, he Emergence of Organized Political ...", pp. 297-8.

25. Documents on the Sudan, 1899-1956, p. 90.

26. Albino, *Sudan: Southern View point,* pp. 30-2.

27. Oduho, *The Problem of Southern Sudan,* pp. 20-3.

28. Ibid., p. 21.

29. Edgar O'balance, *The Secret War in the Sudan: 1955-1972,* (Conncticut: Archon Books, 1977), p. 36.

30. Collins, *Shadow in the Grass,* p. 445.

31. Ibid,. p. 446.

32. Woodward. "The South in the Sudanese Politics, 1946-1956". pp. 178-92; Collins, *Shadows in the Grass,* p. 446.

33. Beshir Mohammed Said, *The Sudan: Crossroads of Africa,* (London: The Bodley Head, 1965), pp. 72-80.

34. Ducan, *The Sudan: A Record of achievement,* pp. 260-78.

35. Holt, *History of the Sudan,* pp. 159-61.

36. Alier, "The Question of the Southern Sudan", pp. 11-27.

37. Documents on the Sudan, 1899-1956, p. 100.

38. Albino, *Sudan; Southern Viewpoint,* pp. 31-76.

39. Henderson, *Sudan Republic,* p. 202.

40. Collins, *Shadow in the Grass,* p. 448.

41. Ibid., p. 437.

42. Albino, *Sudan: Southern Viewpoint,* pp. 28-35.

43. Cecil Epril, *War and Peace in the Sudan, 1955-1972,* (London: David and Charles, 1974), pp. 19-21.

44. Throughout this chapter the two names, 'Southern Liberal party' and the 'Liberal party' will be use interchangeably, with emphasis on the former name. See Wassara, "The Emergence of the Organized Political ...", p. 298.

45. O'balance, *The Secret War in The Sudan*, pp. 36-8.

46. Oduho, *The Problem of the Southern Sudan*, pp. 24-31. It is difficult to find documents containing the lists of members of the party at this stage. Most of the liberal party leaders were scattered allover the South, hence each has his own files. Those who were in the capital did not have an official office to keep their documents.

47. The Report of the Electral Commission, (Khartoum December 13, 1953), p. 4.

48. Holt, *History of the Sudan*, pp. 160-61.

49. Documents on the Sudan, 1899-1953, pp. 12-24.

50. Ibid., pp. 11-14.

51. Said, *The Sudan: Crossroads of Africa*, pp. 72-84.

52. Wassara, "The Emergence of Organized Political Leadership ...", p. 299

53. Henderson, *Sudan Republic*, pp. 172-73.

54. The Report of Electral Commission, pp. 12-20; it is reported that during the election campaign the Egyptian media, especially the 'Radio Cairo' had opened six hours program broadcasting in six Southern Sudanese local languaes.

55. Holt, *The History of the Sudan*. p. 161.

56. Daly, *Imperial Sudan*, p. 264.

57. Beshir, *Southern Sudan: Background to Conflict*, p. 72.

58. Collins, *Shadows in the Grass*, p. 454.

59. Report of the Commission of Inquiry on the Disturbances in Southern Sudan, August 1955, Khartoum, October 1956, pp. 107-114.

60. Wassara, "The Emergence of Organized Political ---", p. 301.

61. Collins, Shadows in the Grass, p. 456.

62. Woodward, *The Sudan, 1898-1989:The Unstable State*, pp. 89-90.

63. Albino, *The Sudan: Southern Viewpoint*, p. 35; Woodward, *The Sudan, 1898-1989*, pp. 90-91; Woodward, "The South in the Sudanese Politics", pp. 178-92; Beshir, *Southern Sudan: Background to Conflict*, p. 73; Gabriel Warburg, *Egypt and Sudan: Studies in History and Politics*, (Frank Cass & Co., 1985), pp. 220-34; Albino, *The Sudan: Southern*

Viewpoint, p. 39; Deng Awour Wenyin, *Southern sudan and the Making of Permanent Constitution in the Sudan*, (Khartoum: University of Juba, 1987), pp. 11-13; also see Oduho, *The Problem of the Southern Sudan*, p. 35; this was the last time the Bloc Members of the parliament participated in the House deliberations before the military coup of November 1958; see Wassara, "The Emergence of Organized Political ...", p. 301. During its life time the Liberal Party preserved a degree of cohesiveness vis-avis the Northern political parties; however, some Southern politicians, for personal reasons, chose to join the Northern parties. Tribal affiliation developed at later stage as we shall see in the next chapter; see Dustan M. Wai, *African-Arab Conflict in the Sudan*, (New York; African Publishing Company, 1981), p. 75.

CHAPTER THREE

The Emergence of Southern Sudanese Political Parties: 1958-70

~

The Federal Party

As discussed earlier, the Federalist Party was created as a reaction to the dissatisfaction of the young Southern Sudanese, mostly intellectuals in the national capital, to the constant rivalry and the continuous floor crossing of the liberal partisans to the competing Northern parties. The federalists decision to establish a separate political organization did not necessarily meant that they doubted the nationalistic stand of the liberals in Southern Sudan issues, rather they felt that the liberals had fought enough and had reached a stage of frustration.

The Founder of the Federal Party was a Shell Company official, Ezbon Mondiri Gwanza, who in 1957, along with other

Southern intellectuals and university graduates, decided to form a party, which should bear the name of the Southern demand. The architect of the new party was a graduate of Faculty of Arts of the University of Khartoum, who before his graduation was an active member in the Southern Student's Welfare Front.[1]

The draft USA-Pattern constitution of the Federal Party included:[2]

1. Federal constitution in the Sudan where Southern and Northern Federal states form relations on equal grounds.
2. The constitution of the Federal Government should be secular;
3. Judicial and executive laws should be regulated and should conform to each federal state's legislative laws.
4. Both English and Arabic should have equal recognition as the two main official languages of the Federal Sudan.
5. Likewise, Christianity and Islam should be recognized as the two major religions in the country without withstanding the right of individuals who believe in other beliefs or religions.
6. The South should have a separate civil service, in which government employment will be the work of southern Federal authorities and subject to its laws and constitution.
7. In order to preserve its cultural identity, the South should have its own educational system at all levels; a Southern university was to be instituted, to be regulated by the Southern Federal Government.

8. The immediate return to the South the three Southern
   secondary schools: Rumbek, Juba commercial school and
   Maridi Teacher-Training centre. The three schools were
   transferred to Khartoum following the 1955 Torit mutiny.[3]
9. Rapid independent economic development program for
   the South.
10. The transfer of the Sudan from Arab world to the African
    world.
11. Creation of independent Southern army.

The party was to achieve these objections, which were considered by the Northern Sudanese to aim at separation, through
cooperation with Southern Liberal Party and with the Eastern
and Western Sudanese political groupings. The founders of
the Federal Party believed that these two regions shared the
idea and often worked toward the establishment of federal
system in the country.

As for the federalists, they considered themselves better
educated and more politically militant and pragmatic in
approach than the old Southern guards.[4] It was with this
understanding that the federalists contested the February
1958 elections. Their candidates and sympathizers were able
to return 40 members of the 43 seats allocated to the South. As
discussed earlier, the federalists' victory brought into parliament a militant united Southern political group. However,
the leader of the Federal Party, Ezbon Mondiri, who secured
a parliamentary seat, was imprisoned for seven years, before
taking his seat, accused for sedition.[5]

The first move toward attainment of its goal, and in order to rally regional support, the Federal Party parliamentarians (now under umbrella of the Southern Parliamentary Bloc) toured the Western and Eastern Sudan regions. Their aim was to lobby for a Federal system of government in the country. This was the first serious attempt by Southerners to rally support to their demands by trying to convince the other 'mergainalized' regions to stand with them.

Contacts with the Beja chiefs were made on 13 August 1958, while in Kordufan and Darfur provinces visits were completed between September and October.[6] Inside the southern Parliamentary Bloc, the Federal-Liberal alliance was strengthened. Their last show with the Northern parliamentarians was when they walked out in the parliament on 16 June 1958 as has be discussed earlier.

In their reaction to the formation and the demands of the Federal Party, the Northern parties argued that the major Nilotic tribes (Nuer, Dinka, Shiluk, Annuak etc.) had little in common with Equatoria politicians (Moru, Azande, Lotuka, Bari etc.), hinting to the composition of the Federal Party's support base. They further reasoned that the would-be federal state in South, if ever established, would not be financially viable without Northern aid. They added that if proper use of the present 'democratic institutions' in terms of establishing a strong program of developing resources of the South with Northern finance, it would give the South what they called "a chance to gain far more than it ever could hope to achieve by bargaining on the basis of independence".[7] The federalists were not surprised by such reaction since it had always been the Northern Sudanese stand to equate federalism with separation.

By and large, the federalists were described as the first Southern Sudanese leaders to advocate for a more radical, militant and serious conscious and coordination with the intellectuals of the Western and Eastern regions. These constructive contacts resulted in that both government and the parliament could not obtain the required quorum to pass the Islamic-unitary Constitution, tabled before the parliament in June 1958. As already pointed out, having failed to implement their plan, the Umma led coalition government handed over the government to the military on 17 November 1958.

Thus, the emergence of the Southern Federal Party was an attempt from the young Southern to take over the responsibility from the old Southern leadership, whose frustration, dissatisfaction and personal clashes had weakened the Southern Liberal Party.[8] However, with the advent of the military dictatorial rule, the Federal Party, together with other political organizations in the country, went into obscurity. The federalists were to reappear six years later under a new name, the Southern Front Party.

The Southern Sudan Organizations in Exile
Sudan African National Union (SANU)
With the parliamentary life brought into an end by the military rule, the Southern political presence in the capital, Khartoum was also suppressed. By 1959, many Southern civil servants

and former parliamentarians were either arrested or fled the country. In December 1960, it was alleged that a big plot to arrest all the remaining Southern politicians was disclosed. Out of fear of arrest or persecution, a considerable number of Southern politicians who were in the South at the time crossed to East Africa. Those who fled to Leopold Ville (Kinshasa), included: Joseph H. Oduho, Ferdinand Adiang, Fr. Saturnino Lohure, Nathaniel Oyet, Pancrasio Ochieng, Marko Rume, Alexis Mbale Yongo and a year later, they were joined by William Deng Nhial, who fled from Kapeota where he was working as Assistant Administrative Commissioner.[9]

Meanwhile, the majority of Southern politicians who did not manage to go to the South either got arrested or went into hiding. Those parliamentarians who were arrested and sentenced were: Ezbon Mondiri Gwanza; sentenced to ten years; Dominic Muorwell, ten years, released in September 1962; James Jokweth, five years; Kamillo Dhol Kuach, three years; Samuel Renzi, five years banishment; Omer Suleiman Lado, seven years; and Lugihit Lokos a tribal chief, seventeen years.[10] It is to be pointed out that most of the arrests occurred in Equatoria where the level of political activity and consciousness was higher compared to Upper Nile and Bahr al-Ghazal provinces. Civil servants whose political intentions were suspected were either arrested or transferred to the North.

Discussing the Southern political activities in exile, one observes a unique character of then emerging political organization. Indeed, what distinguishes the Southern Sudan resistance movement from its counterparts in Africa is that the former began with armed struggle without an organized political wing. In other words, it was an armed resistance than a mass revolutionary movement in which a popular support was lacking in its initial stages in 1950s.[11] It was not until December 1960 that an initiative was taken by the politicians in exile to form a Southern political organization, after six years since the Torit mutiny of 1955.

The pioneers of this organization were Joseph H. Oduho, Aggrey Jaden, Fr. Saturnino Lohure and Alexi Mbale Yongo, all of who were from Equatoria. These four politicians, along with other activists formed the "Sudan Christian Association" or SCA in 1961, in Kampala, Uganda. The creation of this organization was to enlist the support of Foreign Christian organizations both morally and materially. The name was carefully chosen to hide the main political objective of the movement. In fact, it was feared that the hosting country, Uganda, would stop the activities of the organization, had its objectives been clearly stated. It was also the intention of the founders to impress on the idea of religious persecution of Southern Sudanese by the Muslim regime in Khartoum.[12]

A year later in February 1962, the SCA leadership decided to formed a representative political organization. The new organization was to compose all Southern Sudan ethnic group-ings and to be the sole representative of Southern Sudanese in exile. The new organization was called, "Sudan African Closed Districts National Union" or SACDNU. Its headquarters was based in Kinshasa Zaire.[13] The organizational structure of the organization was set; its constitution framed, and the Executive Committee was formed as follows:

Fr. Saturnino Lohure, Patron

Joseph H. Oduho, President

Marko Rume, Vice President

William Deng Nhial, Secretary General

Aggrey Jaden, Deputy Secretary General

The new organization launched its activities and began to consolidate its presence in exile, especially among the southern Sudanese refugees and students abroad. However, in order to accommodate the new politicians who decided to join the movement, the SACDNU leadership met in Kampala, Uganda, on December 25, 1963, where in an informal celebration the name of the organization was changed to "Sudan African National Union" or simply SANU. Later on in the evening of that day they agreed and endorsed the formation of the Executive Committee of SANU as follows:

Fr. Saturnino Lohure: Patron

Joseph H. Oduho: President

Dominic Mourwell: Vice President

Aggrey Jaden: Deputy resident

William Deng Nhial: Secretary General

Pancrasio Ochiang: Treasurer

Valeriario Orget: Deputy Treasurer

Philip Pedak Lieth: Member

Marko Rume: Member

James Wek Achian: Member

Akuot Atem De Mayen: Member

Alexi Mbale Yongo: Member

Banzia Renzi: Member

Nathaniel Oyet Member

The initial activities of SANU, among other things, were to include the following:[14]

Fundraising and securing international recognition and for that purpose in 1963, Oduho and Fr. Lohure made their first tour to Europe, which led them also to Vatican. William Deng Nhial, the Secretary General took similar visits to Europe.

SANU leadership published a propaganda paper in French with title "the Southern Sudan Liberation Movement," apparently translated from a similar paper in English in which the objective of the movement was declared to be independence of the Southern Sudan sovereign state. The information office of the movement published and circulated in 1962 a magazine called *The Voice of the Southern Sudan* in London, its publication ceased in June 1964.

In the summer of 1963, Joseph H. Oduho and William Deng Nhial co-authored in the name of the organization *The Problem of Southern Sudan*, which remained to be the first comprehensive published work covering different aspects of the problem of the Southern Sudanese at the time.

While maintaining the peaceful means of solving the problem, SANU leaders began to organize secretly guerilla bands within the Southern Sudan. The organization's secretariat petitioned the United Nations, United States of America and later on the organization of African Unity, OAU.

In addition to the tours in Europe, other members went to visit African countries where they explained to the African leaders the aims of SANU. It is to be noted that, as earlier as May 1962, other members took initiatives to mobilize Southerners inside the country. One of the activists who exerted efforts towards that direction was Marko Rume, who wrote several letters to the Southern Sudanese in Equatoria urging them to join the movement. He asked government employees to quite their jobs, warning them of a possible invasion of Southern Sudan by the Northern troops. He urged students to leave their schools and leave the country for the possible reprisals by the Northern army.15 Certainly not most of what Rume said in his letters necessarily described what was actually happening; yet his letters had enormous effect on those who had a chance to read them. Inside the country the news of SANU's activities reached all the corners of the South. Some activists decided to work in secret mobilizing and enlisting moral and sometimes material support to the liberation movement. However, for security reasons, the three leaders of SANU (Joseph Oduho, Aggrey Jaden and William Deng) were simply referred to as "The Trio".16

The political atmosphere, in which SANU was formed, did not help in making it a national united movement. Diversity in views, personality clashes, and personal ambition for power soon surfaced. This was true as far as the coordination and cooperation among the executive committee members was concerned. William Deng for example, chose to stay in Kinshasa while the rest of the Executive Committee members remained in the headquarters in Kampala.[17] Another issue was that the personalities of Joseph Oduho, William Deng and Fr. Saturnino Lohure were such that it was difficult for the three men to work together. In fact, none of them found it necessarily to be accountable to the SANU Executive Committee, let alone to the President of the Organization. Each viewed himself as a leader not restricted by authority; however the three were individually, at least, committed to the Southern cause.[18]

The first quarrels among the SANU Executive Committee members came into surface on the naming of the military of the wing of the movement. Several names were suggested. Among these were 'South Sudan Land Freedom Army', SSLFA; 'Azania Secret Army', ASA; 'AnyaNya', which was suggested by Joseph Oduho and Joseph Lagu; and 'Sudan Pan-African Freedom Fighters, SPAFF, suggested by Fr. Saturnino, but rejected outright on the ground that it does not connect the movement with Southern Sudan.[19] The disagreements among SANU leaders over the naming of the movement was illustrated by a letter addressed to Joseph Oduho by William Deng, criticizing the former by saying:

> *"If by your contention you mean to say that 'AnyaNya' is the official name, then it should have been discussed by SANU executive, (and) since it has not been discussed, the three names, ASA, SSLFA and AnyaNya remain unofficial and should be left to the Armed Forces who are directly concerned...If SSLFA is adopted as the official name, I can not see*

how it can divide the South anymore than can ASA
and AnyaNya...Name may not divide but actions
such as yours can."[20]

From the above quotation, it is implied that the two men did not agree, not only on the name, even on the methodology used to decide on the name. William Deng's opponents argued that he could not have accepted other name than the one he suggested, nor could he accept a compromise that would not take into consideration his version. To his antagonists he was incline to make arbitrary decisions in the name of SANU without proper consultations, which apparently upset many of his colleagues with whom he was invariably in disagreement.[21]

Despite these disagreements the party leadership began its contacts wit the Southern Sudanese refugees in East Africa, urging them to support the movement. However, being hosted by a country whose good relations with Khartoum government were rapidly growing, the Ugandan authorities detained Joseph Uduho, the President of SANU in February 1964.[22] In order to avoid more deterioration, Joseph Oduho managed to gather most of the Executive Committee members and other Southern Sudanese politicians in exile to attend a general national convention in Uganda. The convention was actually held between 7 and 16 November 1964 in Kampala, in absence of the Secretary General William Deng, who was at the time in European tour. After serious deliberations, a 'Shadow Cabinet' was elected and the posts of President and Secretary General were abolished. The election gave the top positions to:[23]

Aggrey Jaden, President
Fr. Saturnino Lohure, Patron
Philip Pedak Lieth, Vice President
William Deng Nhial, Secretary General
Dominic Mourwell: Secretary for Special Affairs
Joseph H. Oduho, Secretary for Legal and Constitutional
Affairs
Elia Lupe, Secretary of Interior
Goerge Kwanai, Secretary for Information
Michael Wal Duany, Secretary for Finance
Lawrence Wol Wol, Secretary for Education
Oliver Albino, Secretary for Refugee Affairs

Having clearly admitted the existence of personal and tribal conflicts in the movement, Aggrey Jaden told his colleagues in his speech that:

> *"At this stage of our movement it is now absolutely important, more than ever that we need Unity of aims. To be united does not mean to abolish differences of opinion or point of view...but it is very necessary that we must be united in our common and final goal which is independence from the North...we must try to bury our personal, tribal and sectional interests for the sake of our beloved country... only Unity will be our strength."*[24]

The November 1964 convention left out William Deng from

its Executive Committee; it also demoted Joseph Oduho who had shown his reservation in the process, but chose to wait and see. The basic achievements of the convention were:[25]

1. For the first time the objective of the movement was clearly declared;

2. It was the first time that the Southern liberation moment's leadership was democratically elected;

3. The Kampala convention announced the appointment, for the first time, of diplomatic representatives to be responsible as emissaries of SANU shadow government abroad. Representative to United States of America, Britain, Former USSR, Tanzania, Kenya, Zaire, Central African Republic and Ethiopia, were appointed,

4. The draft Constitution for the Movement was prepared.

Moreover, the movement tried to solve internal problems, within its ranks and tried to influence the military wing of the movement. By and large, the convention had shown the willingness and possibility of uniting Southern Sudanese leadership and masses along national lines. However, individual efforts to remedy the personal clashes among the movement's leadership, or to reform the movement itself were not successful.

The following are excerpts from a letter addressed to William Deng by Oliver Battali Albino in which the later complained about the lack of cooperation:

"I have lost all hopes in the reorganization of SANU itself. Tribalism and regionalism are obviously being sustained to enhance individual ambitions...

Another discouraging attitude to those who would
work for reorganization is that 'this is SANU which
we formed, if you like it join us, if you don't, then
start your own party and let us see'... The present
leadership (Aggrey's) are partly responsible for our
people's sufferings because disunity among us is
what the Arabs are working for. "[26]

In October 1964 a popular uprising overthrown the military government in Khartoum. The SANU leadership was sharply divided over what policies it would take to deal with the new changes inside the country.[27]

SANU and the Round Table Conference March 1965
The civilian caretaking government of Sirr Al Khatim Khalifa, announced on November 14th, 1964 an uncondi-tional Amnesty for all Southerners who had fled the country since 1955, including those sentenced by courts in absentia. He further urged Southerners in exile to put aside all racial, religious and political differences and asked them to return home. Most importantly, he made an offer to Southern leaders, which amounted to 'Federal Autonomy'.[28] The first Southern reaction to the Prime Ministers' announcement came from William Deng Nhial, who at the time in Europe, wrote a letter to the Prime Minister, on his capacity as SANU's Secretary General, in November 1964.[29]

Having expressed his willingness to return to the country William put the following conditions:[30]

1. That a general amnesty to be declared by the government for all refugees.
2. That SANU be recognized as a political party to contest the forthcoming elections on the policy of a Federal Sudan.
3. That a written guarantee by the government deposited with the Secretary General of OAU, that none of the refugees and SANU leaders will be victimized.
4. That a round-table conference between all Sudanese political parties with representatives from the Judiciary, the University of Khartoum, the Trade Unions, observers from Arab and African countries, and the secretariat of OAU, be convened to discuss the general lines of working relationship between North and South.
5. Accept the fact that the Sudan is Afro-Arab state with two distinct cultures, Negriod and Arab. Unity in diversity is the answer to the Southern problem and this can be found in a federal constitution.

On December 10th, 1964, the Prime Minister, in response to William Deng's letter, proposed a round-table conference to be held in Juba on February 6th, 1965. However, upon hearing the Prime Minister's proposal, the 'AnyaNya' forces intensified their military activities around Juba, ignoring William's appeal.31 Disillusioned by William's unilateral proposal to accept federal status for the South, and in order to hide internal differences, the SANU Executive Committee held a meeting in Kampala, on January 20th, 1965, in which it announced that a three-man committee be formed; it composed of William Deng Nhial, Michael Wal Duany and Elia Lupe. The committee drawn up the conditions under which SANU was prepared to negotiate, what included:[32]

1. SANU undertakes to appeal to all Southern Sudanese to call off fighting throughout the Southern Sudan; and that the state of emergency be lifted in the south.
2. The government undertakes to ensure the safety of all negotiating parties and the state of emergency inside the Juba city is lifted.
3. Local and international press shall be invited to follow the negotiations.
4. SANU members of the delegation shall be free to go back to report the results of the negotiations to SANU members in exile.
5. The conference should find a solution to the problem of Southern Sudan.

Upon the receipt of SANU's conditions the government and the newly formed 'Southern Front Party' sent delegations to East Africa in an attempt to convince the SANU leaders to come to Khartoum, since Juba has already become a security risk. Convinced by the Southern Front's third delegation, William Deng Nhial flew to Khartoum on February 27th, 1965 accompanied by six politicians. On his arrival in Khartoum, William Deng was asked by a journalist 'why are your people (SANU leaders) causing all this trouble?' 'Who are they?' William Deng answered: "I do not know who they are".[33]

Meanwhile, Aggrey Jaden's group remained adamant that since Juba was insecure, the meeting should take place abroad. Already William Deng have informed the government that he was representing SANU, and argued that since the idea of round-table conference was first initiated by him, there was no reason to bother about the other groups who refused to return home. In fact, the government could have welcomed a boycott of the conference by Jaden's delegation had they not accepted to attend, a move which could have forced the government to recognize William Deng's group officially, and perhaps persuaded him to take a solution less than federation.[34]

When Jaden's faction accepted to attend the conference, the next move was how to incorporate William Deng's faction into a united SANU delegation. After a bitter discussion, mediated by the southern Front, Jaden's Faction was persuaded to accept William as a member of a united SANU delegation. He ranked the sixth among SANU nine delegates. A compromise was also reached in which William Deng's group will have four representatives and Jaden extremist group would send five and the chair of the delegation should go to Jaden's group. The SANU's delegation was led by Elia Lupe with membership of:[35]

Elia Lupe,
Lawrence Wol Wol,
George Akumbek Kwanai,
Oliber B. Albino,
George Lomoro,
William Deng Nhial,
Hilary Ukalla Akuono,
Nikanora M. Aguer
Elia Duang

Insisting to be the leader of SANU, and delivered his speech as such, William Deng's position throughout the conference remained obscure. In a communiqué and statements the government had to be deliberately vague about his actual status in the conference. In general, he seemed to be happy with it. The Southern Front delegation to the conference was led by its Vice President Gordon Mourtat, Mayen, it included:

Abel Alier Kuay,
Gordon Abiei,
Othwonh Dak,
Othwonh Buogo,
Natale Olwak,
Lubari Ramba,
Bona Malwal Ring,
Domano Hassan.

Both SANU and Southern Front rejected the representation of the revived Liberal Party, Ramadan Chol's Sudan Peace Party, and the Sudan Unity Party of Philmon Majok and Santino Deng (not related to William Deng).[36]

On the other hand, the Northern parties insisted that those Southerners, whose views were not in line with those of Southern Front or SANU, should be represented. As a compromise, a group, referred to as 'Other Shades of Opinion or OSO', were selected by the Ministry of Local Government, they were:[37]

Philemon Majok, Former MP, Bahr Al-Ghazal;
Ring Lual, Sultan, Bahr al-Ghazal;
James Bol Kalmal; Sudan Tobacco Co., Upper Nile;

Edward Amum, Sultan, Upper Nile;

Gordon Soro, Town Clerk Equatoria Province;

Charles Ati Bilal, Former MP; Equatoria;

Yousuf Duku, Sultan, Equatoria Province.

In addition, six Northern delegates, led by their Presidents and Secretary Generals, attended the conference, they were:

Sadik al-Mahdi, Umma Party,

Ali Abdel Rahaman, People's Democratic Party,

Abdel Khaliq Mahjoub, Sudan Communist Party,

Hassan Abdalla Turabi, Islamic Charter Front,

Mekkawi Mustafa, Professional Front,

Ismail Ahmed El-Azhari, National Unionist Party,

The conference was chaired by Professor Nazir Daffalla, Chancellor of Khartoum University, assisted by Professor Mohamed Omer Beshir, academic secretary of Khartoum University. In presence of observers from Algeria, Egypt, Ghana, Kenya, Nigeria, Tanzania and Uganda, the Round-Table Conference was opened on 16th-25th March 1965 by the Prime Minister. In unexpected move, the 'Nine Other Shades of Opinion' declared their support to SANU and the Southern Front objectives, and moved to sit next to the two delegates inside the conference. The move certainly embarrassed the Northern parties delegates.[38]

The Prime Minister, Sirr al-Khatim, in his inaugural speech, which was prepared by the secretariat, gave a rather lengthy and somehow apologetic outline to the problem, blaming the British for all the ills of the country and partially blamed the military regime and political parties. He urged the delegates to reach a peaceful solution to the problem.[39] In his speech, William Deng stated that the only possible compromise was the establishment of American type federal system, which in details not very much different from the one proposed by the Northern parties. The latter's proposal was system of 'local government', in which national unity would by maintained.[40]

Southern Front's Vice President demanded self-determination in which, if accepted by the conferees, a plebiscite in the south would be conducted to give Southerners a chance to decide whether they wanted unconditional unity, Local Government, federation or secession. This proposal was rejected outright by Northern Sudanese parties who considered it another version of separation.[41]

The speech of SANU faction was delivered by its leader Aggrey Jaden, who explained in length the history of South-North relations with emphasis on the history of slavery. He concluded by saying that it was in the interests of the two regions to separate peacefully. He added:

> *"...The Sudan falls sharply in two distinct areas, both in geographical area, ethnic groups and cultural systems.*
>
> *The Northern Sudan is occupied by a hybrid race, who were united by their common language, common culture, and common religion, and they look to the Arab world for their cultural and political inspiration. The people of the Southern Sudan on the other hand, belong to the African ethnic group*

of East Africa...They do not only differ from the hybrid Arab race in origin, but in all conceivable purposes...There is nothing in common between the various sections of the community nobody of shared beliefs, no identity of interests, no local signs of unity and above all the Sudan has failed to compose a single community... There could be no settlement of differences until separation and independence had been granted to the South... Apart from posing a threat to African peace, the Southern problem has seeds of damaging Afro-Arab relations... To avoid this, the Southern Sudan must be given its own independence, if further damage be avoided."[42]

Aggrey Jaden also pointed out in his speech inequality of the central government in all aspects (refer to tables, 8, 9, and 10).

Table 8

Government Secondary Schools for Boys in the Sudan up to 1965

	Number of Schools in the North	Number of Schools in the South
Before the Independence	4	2
Added after Independence	18	None
Total	22	2

Source: Albino, *The Sudan: Southern Viewpoint, p. 100.*

Table 9

Intake to the Sudan Police College

Year	No. of Northerners	No. of Southerners
1950	10	3
1951	14	4
1953	13	7
1957	27	3
1960	29	none
1961	36	1
1963	26	1
1964	35	2
Total	190	21

Source: *Albino, The Sudan: Southern Viewpoint, p. 104.*

Table 10

Office Commissioned in the Sudanese Army

Date	No. of Southerners	No. of Northerners
27.7.1954	1	19
1.8.1955	3	45
1.4.1955	3	35
1.7.1957	3	40
1.5.1958	2	58
1.5.1959	1	56
1.5.1960	2	58
1.1.1962	none	64
1.1.1963	1	56
1.1.1964	none	71
1.1.1965	4	7
Total	20	569

Source: Albino, *The Sudan: Southern Viewpoint, p. 105.*

The failure of the Round-Table Conference could be attributed to:
1. The Southern opinion was divided.
2. The pressures exerted by the AnyaNya forces, obliged Jaden's faction not to accept any proposal short of separation.
3. The Northern parties were more concerned with the forthcoming elections, than with negotiating peace with a divided Southern delegates.

4. Northern politicians, and to some extend the public, were appalled by the mistrust the Southerners expressed in the conference. Their mistakes were pointed out publicly, and this might have enraged most of them, and some went far as boycotting the conference.[43]

On March 29 1965, the conferees, convinced of the deadlock, they have reached, resolved the following:[44]
1. To adjourn the conference for a period of three months
2. To set up a twelve-man committee to study and recommend constitutional, administrative, and financial relations between the South and the central government
3. An interim crash programme for the South to be carried out.

Once he had delivered his controversial speech, Aggrey Jaden, accompanied by his rival, Joseph Oduho, left for Uganda; the rest of his delegation remained behind, and followed after the conclusion of the conference leaving behind only one member, Oliver B Albino, to represent it in the twelve-man committee. Few days later he joined his leadership in Kampala. On the other hand, William Deng's faction remained in Khartoum and was later on recognized as a political party.45

By and large, the Round Table Conference was instrumental in William Deng's defection. However, despite its failure, the conference did provide an opportunity for the two sides of the conflict to listen to each other's opposing views for the first time since August 1955. However, the most important element of the conference was that the press coverage of the conference helped to enlighten the Northern public opinion about the North-South conflict. Added to this, the presence of the foreign observers in the conference had lifted the Sudanese civil war to an African-Arab scene.[46]

Disunity Among the Southern Sudanese Leaders in Exile, 1965-70

The failure of the Round Table Conference was not only a sad setback to the country as a whole, but also had had negative repercussions to the SANU leadership in exile. Upon their return to Kampala, Aggrey Jaden and Joseph Oduho resumed their old antagonism. It is to be recalled that William Deng and Joseph Oduho were not pleased by November 1964 SANU executive elections. With William Deng already in Khartoum, Oduho saw in failure of the conference a great chance for new elections in the organization. On the other hand, SANU leader, Aggrey Jaden, preferred a status quo if further splits in the movement be avoided. Open and secret mediation and deliberations followed, but all went in vain. Consequently, Joseph Oduho and his supporters defected from SANU in June 1965 and formed their own secessionist organization, which they called "Azania Liberation Front, ALF." In a statement in which they announced the creation of the new front, the ALF leaders promised to unite the movement's military and political wings. They made the liberation of southern Sudan from Khartoum government as their main objective. Leaving his residence in Kampala, Fr. Saturnino Lohure joined Oduho group and moved into Southern Sudan where he made Tul his headquarters. The Executive Committee of ALF was composed of:[47]

Joseph H. Oduho: President

Fr. Saturnino Lohure: Vice President

Ezbon Mondiri Gwanza: Defense Secretary

George Akumbek Kwanai: Foreign Secretary

Joseph Lagu Yanga: Commander-in-Chief

William Hassan: Assistant Commander-in-Chief

Elia Lupe: Member

Pancrasio-Ochiang: Member

Marko Rume: Member

In order to consolidate his authority over the "AnaNya' army throughout the South, Oduho sent his Defense Secretary Ezbon Mondiri to tour Western Equatoria and Bahr al-Ghazal. Meanwhile, Oduho himself toured Eastern Equatoria, his homeland, where he met with local commanders and explained to them why he had defected from SANU. Believing that power lies with the military, it was Oduho's intention to rally the AnyaNya support behind him. The ALF underneath focus on soliciting military support should be seen therefore, as an attempt to coordinate the political leadership and the activities with 'AnyaNya' campaign.[48] Oduho's attempts partially succeeded in Bahr al-Ghazal and in Equatoria, however, his support in Upper Nile province was minimum.

It did not take long time before differences within ALF surfaced. Oduho dismissed Ezbon Mondiri and Elia Lupe accusing them of being secretly cooperating with his rival Aggrey Jaden. On the other hand, personal differences between Oduho and Fr. Saturnino intensified by the mid of July 1965. While on a brief visit to Kampala, Oduho was for the second time detained by the Uganda authorities in July 1965. His arrest coincided with Premier Mohammed Ahmed Mahjoub official visit to Kampala. He was released and left for eastern Equatoria. While in the region, disagreements between Joseph Oduho and his commander-in-chief, Joseph Lagu, reached uncompromising level. In fact, Joseph Oduho was arrested by Colonel Joseph Lagu, who was at the time under patronage of Fr. Saturnino. Oduho was sentenced to death, however, due to his poor health, the death sentence was not carried out. He was released and went to East Africa.[49]

After Oduho's defection, Aggrey Jaden decided to change the name of his faction of SANU and created another organization which he temporarily called 'Sudan African Liberation Front, SALF', maintaining Kampala November 1964 convention resolutions, he kept the top positions of the Executive Committee as they were before Oduho's defection:

Aggrey Jaden: President-General

Dominic Marwell: National Chairman

Philip Pedak Lieth: Vice President

Other politicians who were not satisfied with Oduho or Jaden's leadership formed their own organization, which they called "African Freedom Fighters Union of Conservatives". However, nothing much is known about its programs, its membership or when it was created; but it soon disappeared following the unity of ALF and SALF in August 1965.[50]

With this confused situation, mediation efforts were made
by church leaders, Southern Sudan student unions in exile,
and by the friends of the movement. As a result of these efforts,
a meeting was held in Kampala, Uganda, between 25th-26th
August 1965 attended by both ALF and SALF leadership. After
a lot of deliberations, a joint communiqué of reconciliation
was released on 28th August 1965. The communiqué among
other things, agreed on the following resolutions:[51]

1. The members of SANU (Jaden's SALF and Oduho's
   ALF) have agreed under the new name of Sudan African
   Liberation Front (SALF).
2. Under the conclusion of unity the two organizations have
   agreed to relinquish their former names, SANU and ALF.
3. The two organizations have agreed on common aim of total
   independence for the Southern Sudan and on the common
   policy of applying force to achieve this end.
4. The two organizations agreed to support the AnyaNya as
   an individual body before and after the achievement of
   independence.
5. The two organizations have agreed to adopt the leadership of SANU for the new organization:
   Dominic Mourwell, National Chairman;
   Aggrey Jaden, President
   Philip Pedak Lieth, Vice President.
6. On the foreign policy the new organization had this to
   say:[52]

       i The SALF condemns the Arab Northern Sudan and
   their bid to perpetuate Arab domination over the South.

ii   Condemn the Arab line-up comprising Algeria, Egypt (UAE), Syria and Jordan in supporting the Khartoum Arabs in their atrocities.

iii   Also protest strongly against the foreign powers, especially Russia and China who are supporting the Arabs in exterminating the Black African of the Southern Sudan.

iv   Condemn the Western countries who are giving military and financial aid to the Arabs of the Northern Sudan.

The August 1965 meeting was certainly a victory to Aggrey Jaden, who managed to convince the attendants that unity could be maintained if the leadership of the movement is stable.

However, it was not long when the two men, Aggrey Jaden and Joseph Oduho, broke away each reviving his old organization. Among other peace loving groups, Dr. Justo Muludiang, Dr. Lawrence Wol Wol and George M. Lomoro, took an initiative to reconcile the two leaders. The three mediators were however, Oduho's supporters who were also representatives of the Southern liberation movement in Europe. They argued that the leadership of the movement should be stable. They added that Joseph Oduho was well known in Europe following his tour there in early 1960's. The new reconciliation was made in December 1965, this time on expense of Aggrey's leadership.

According to the new agreement, Joseph Oduho became President and Aggrey Jaden Vice President. The two leaders

agreed that the new name for the organization would be ALF –
A new constitution was drafted. Its preamble read as follows:

> *"We the African people, owners and masters of the*
> *country presently known as the Southern Sudan*
> *victimized by the perpetuation of political, cultural*
> *and economic domination and oppression and all*
> *forms of colonial policies and practices which had*
> *been wrecked by African continent... have therefore*
> *formulated and bound ourselves to this constitution*
> *for the sole aim of liberating the Southern Sudan*
> *and establishing a free and independent African*
> *nation so that the black man in this part of the conti-*
> *nent may realize security, justice, welfare and his*
> *hitherto lost human rights and dignity."*[53]

The uneasiness between the two men remained unresolved,
each finding it difficult to recognize the leadership of another.
By 1967, many peace loving people failed to remedy the confusion in the Southern Sudan leadership. Tribalism, regionalism
and individual rivalry became the reign of the time. Accusing
him of having met secretly with William Deng, who was on a
visit to Nairobi, Joseph Oduho dismissed Aggrey Jadaen from
ALF. He charged him of insubordination.

Aggrey Jaden left ALF and formed yet another ogranization
of his own. He called it this time "Home Front, HF". Early in
1967, a group of Aggrey Jaden's supporters decided to transfer
the Southern political movement from exile to Lomiliria in

Equatoria province. Later on in the year, the headquarters of the organization was transferred to Anguri, near the Sudan-Zaire border.54 On the other hand, the continued rivalry among political leaders of the movement had weakened the whole liberation movement. Thus, the military wing of the movement decided to interfere in order to rescue the movement from eminent collapse. On this ground a national convention was called, in which both the military and all the Southern political organization in exile attended. The venue of the meeting was Anguri, the new headquarters of the movement.

The Southern Sudan Provisional Government, SSPG

1. In presence of politicians and the AnyaNya commanders, the Anguri Convention was opened on 15th-18th August 1967. The Agenda of the Convention were discussed. Both political and military reforms were explored and the following resolutions were passed:[55]

2. The 'National Government' was formed and named 'Southern Sudan Provisional Government, SSPG'.

3. The Convention passed a resolution transferring the political headquarters of the movement from exile to the bush in the Southern Sudan.

4. All other political organizations were dissolved and both the military and political wings were united.

5. The First National Flag was created.

6. The Convention decreed that there should be an annual and regular convention of this kind.

On foreign policy, the Convention resolved that:[56]

1. The SSPG look forward for close cooperation with Liberation Movements in Africa (SWAPO, PRELIMO, ANC, MPLA, ZANU etc.).
2. Liberation of Southern Sudan from Arab rule
3. Opposition to communism, imperialism and racism;
4. Support for all international peace movements, World Council of Churches, all African Congress of Churches and Sudan Council of Churches.
5. Support for a greater East African common market; opposition to religious or racial prejudices or discrimination among members and supporters of the SSPG; and with this understanding the desire to negotiate and cooperate with any Arab government.

The Convention formed the provisional government composed of a political bureau and executive council:

Political Bureau
Aggrey Jaden, President
Camilio Dhol Kwac, Vice President
Francis Mayer, Attorney General
Severino Fulli, Minister for Presidential Affairs

Executive Council

Name	Position	Province	Tribe
Aggrey Jaden	President	Eqatoria	Pojulu
Akuot Atem De Mayen	Defense	Upper Nile	Dinka
Elia Lupe	Interior	Equatoria	Kakw
Gordon M Mayen	Foreign Affairs	Bahr al-Ghazal	Dinka
Othwanh Dak	Education	Upper Nile	Shiluk
Gabriel Kao	Justice	Bahr al-Ghazal	Dinka
George A Kwanai	Information	Upper Nile	Shiluk
Lawrence Wol Wol	Agriculture	Bahr al-Ghazal	Dinka
Joseph H. Oduho	Communication	Equatoria	Lotuko
Elia Duag	Animal & Natural Resources	Bahr al-Ghazal	Dinka
David Koak Goak	Social & Refugees Affairs	Upper Nile	Nuer
Tadio Pedit	Finance & Economics	Bahr al-Ghazal	Dinka

In a move to implement the resolutions of the Anguri Convention, the headquarters of the SSPG was transferred to Bungu, in Western Equatoria, near Yei District. AnyaNya forces were renamed 'AnyaNya National Armed Forces,

ANAF'. The ANAF was nominally brought under civil control of the President and the Secretary of Defense. For the first time 'a Defense Council' was formed, composed of President, Secretary of Defense, the Commander-in-Chief, Chief of Staff and Chief of Intelligence. This council was in charge of military operations. The Defense Council delegated powers to each of the three regional commanders in Upper Nile, Equatoria, and Bahr al-Ghazal provinces to direct military operations.[57]

The SSPG's urgent task was to govern and establish an administration in those areas under its control. It was also hoped that it would gain respect and strength, since it was already operating within the South as guerrilla government in the bush. On Civilian Administration, the SSPG took up the proposal forwarded by Ezbon Mondiri in 1965, in which he suggested division of the three Southern provinces into nine administrative regions. Each region was to be ruled by a commissioner, who coordinates his work with his army counterpart. These regional commissioners in turn were responsible to the combined 'military and political headquarters', which the SSPG was working hard to become. Moreover, regional, provincial and district councils were created to coordinate military and civilian organizations. The districts were organized into village councils, whose work was to provide recruits that would form what the SSPG called 'Home Guards'. These guards were to protect the villages and districts against accesses of the government army.[58] The diagram below illustrates the military and administrative structure of the SSPG:

The Regional Civil Wing of the AnyaNya Adminstration

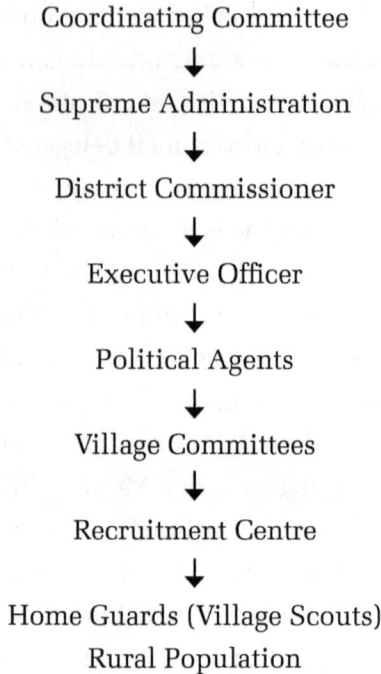

Coordinating Committee
↓
Supreme Administration
↓
District Commissioner
↓
Executive Officer
↓
Political Agents
↓
Village Committees
↓
Recruitment Centre
↓
Home Guards (Village Scouts)
Rural Population

Source: Elias NymLell Wakoson, "The Origins and the Development of the AnyaNya Movement" in Mohamed O. Beshir, *Southern Sudan: Regionalism and Religion* (Khrtoum University Press, 1984), p. 148.

The Convention therefore, has learned lessons from the previous confusion by the politicians and has to some extent revealed that the Southern Sudanese politicians in exile had shown a certain degree of political maturity and responsibility. After the Convention, delegates and special envoys were sent to European and African states urging their leaders to help the southern Liberation Movement.[58]

The Nile Provisional Government NPG

The Major threat that the SSPG faced came from the Zandeland and the Moruland, both in Western Equatoria. In these areas, local commanders rejected the appointment of General Emidio Taffeng as Commander-in-Chief of the AnyaNya. Moreover, Eastern Equatoria, much of Bahr al-Ghazal and all the Upper Nile provinces did not join, in terms of representation, the SSPG as expected. Furthermore, politicians from smaller communities such as Madi, resented what they called 'Dinka Clique' domination.[59]

The first disagreements within the SSPG Executive Council surface between Aggrey Jaden, a Pojulu, and his Foreign Affairs Secretary Godon Mourtat Mayen, a Dinka. The former complained that he was not respected and supported by the latter. He further accused his deputy, Camilio Dhol, a Dinka, of working to depose him. Alarmed by the increased tension, and having failed to convene a national convention, as proposed by the Anguri Convention, Aggrey Jaden decamped to Nairobi, deserting his Presidency.[60] Pressurized by the remaining Executive members, and in order to avoid further defections, the Acting President Camilio Dhol, called for a national Convention at Bulgo-Bindi, near the Sudan-Zaire border.

The Convention was opened on 29th March 1969, having adopted all the Anguri Convention resolutions the Pulgo-Bindi Convention added the following resolutions:[61]

1. The name of the SSPG was changed and the 'Nile Provisional Government, NPG' was adopted with Gordon Mourtat Mayen as the President, and a Republic, the 'Nile State' was declared.
2. Separation from the North was the basic policy, while federation could be accepted as a compromise.
3. The 'AnyaNya' Forces were to persecute the war of liberation
4. The idea of any autonomous status for the South was rejected.
5. The NPG has to work for Southern National Unity and the idea of representative government should be always adopted.

Prior to the convening of the Convention, a series of discussions took place behind the scenes, and several names were proposed:[62]

1. 'Azania State' was turned down because it did not reflect anything connected with Southern Sudan, and in any case it was a small region on the East African Coast.
2. 'Fashoda State' was rejected on the ground that the name was given by the British; moreover, it restricts the geographical representation in the South.
3. 'Nilotia State' was excluded because it reflected ethnic belonging, while not all Southern Sudanese are Nilotes.63
4. The supporters of 'Nile Republic' to be adopted as the official name gave the following justifications:
    i   The movements at this stage have definite goal, to

free Southern Sudan from Northern Sudan, thus, the need to have a name that should have no connection with the word 'Sudan'.

ii The economic potential of the Southern Sudan was based on the Nile. In addition to Papyrus, other resources were considered such as fisheries, hydroelectric power, and transporatation.

iii Geographically all the rivers in the Southern Sudan (Sobat, Bahr al-Jabal, Gilo, Bahr al-Ghazal, the Sue river etc.) pour into the Nile; and all came from all over the Southern Sudan.

At the end of the Convention, the delegates agreed to form a government composing of eight ministers. The top posts went to:[64]

Gordon Mourtat Mayen	President
Marko Rume	Vice President
Archanglo Bari Wangi	Foreign Affairs
General Emidio Taffeng	Commander-in-Chief
Brigidier Emmanuel Abur	Chief of Staff.

Meanwhile, Aggrey Jaden's grouping boycotted the Pulgo-Bindi Convention hence it was not represented. Four of the eight 'ministerial' posts went to Dinka, and this disappointed even some of the NPG's supporters from minority communities. Following its establishment, the very reasons that hindered SSPG's effectiveness faced the NPG Executive Council. Ethnic affiliation and regional belonging undermined the Nile government's attempts to carry out its duties. The

basic hurdle seemed to have been that the majority of the
civil and military members of the government came from Bahr
al-Ghazal and Upper Nile provinces.[65] As a counter action to
this 'Dinka domination' Equatorian minor communities were
prompted to form a number of self-proclaimed Governments:

The Anyidi Revolutionary Government ARG
Following his desertion of SSPG presidency and without his
knowledge, some of Aggrey Jaden's supporters managed to win
over General Emidio Tuffeng, Former Commander-in-Chief
of both the SSPG and NPG. It was Tuffeng's initial idea to
overthrow Gordon from within the Government, but he failed.
Instigated by James Eliyaba Loboka Surrur, a Pojulu, Sarafino
Wani Swaka, a Bari, and with help of nine ANAF officers,
Taffeng announced on September [15th], 1969, the formation of
'Anyidi Revolutionary Government, ARG'. 'Anyidi' was an old
trading post in Western Equatoria. Outlining his main objectives, Taffeng adopted all the resolutions of both Anguri and
Pulgo-Bindi conventions. The top posts of his government
went to:[66]

General Emidio Tuffeng	President
Aggrey Jaden	Foreign Affairs
James Eleyoba Loboka Surrur	Finance and Information
Col. Fedrick Magot	Chief of Staff
Sarafino Wani Swaka	Member

The Sue River Revolutionary Government, SRRG
Disappointed by what they considered to be ineffective

governments, the Azande leaders decided to form their own 'Government' in opposition to both the NPG and ARG. Backed by Colonel Samuel Abu John, a local commander in the area, Michael Tawil formed a government which he called 'Sue River Revolutionary Government, SSRG', and created a state known as the 'Sue Republic'. The sue River flowed northwards from near Yambio, passing through Wau before flowing into the Sudd-Nile. Michael Tawil's establishment was regarded as motivated by ethnic jealousy, since he refused to recognize the authority of NPG, a government he categorized as a 'Dinka organization'.[67] He was to wage the war of liberation without NPG.

The Sudan Azania Government, SAG
About the same time of the SSRG formation, Ezbon Mondiri Gwanza, former founder of the Federal Party and former Defense Secretary of ALF, formed his own government, which he called 'The Sudan Azania Government in East Africa'. Nothing much is known about this government or when it was actually formed, except that Alphonso Malek Parjokdit, a Dinka, was instrumental in formation of the new government. Moreover, like its predecessors, SANU, ALF, SALF, SSPG, NPG, ARG, and SPRG, the Sudan Azania Government was determined to fight for Southern National Unity and independence of Southern Sudan.[68] Despite the ethnic and regional element in all the splits in the Southern leadership in exile in the 1960's, all these governments tried to maintain an element of a representative government. In each government, ethnic belonging was always considered.

By September 1969, there were three 'southern Governments', NPG, ARRG, SRG, and SAG. Inside the country, as will be seen, there were William Deng SANU, the Southern Front Party, the Liberal Party, the Sudan Unity Party and the Sudan Peace Party. Indeed, twenty-three years since the Juba Conference of 1947, a great difference in political awareness in Southern Sudanese leadership took place. The level of political maturity reached during this period, was influenced by ethnic consciousness. One still wonders if the southern leaders of provincial councils, political committees, trade unionists, the liberals and even the SANU leadership, knew what future hided for them.

With this heightened confusion and stalemate, one of the ANAF Commanders, Colonel Joseph Lagu, stationed at the time in Eastern Equatoria in Owiny-Kibul, decided to and succeeded in uniting all the AnyaNya forces leaving politicians with their conflicts. The AnyaNya under him became the sole military and political effective liberation movement in the southern Sudan. He called the new organization 'Southern Sudan Liberation Movement, SSLM'. In the cause of national unity, NPG dissolved itself in July 1970, and all the other Southern governments in exile followed suit and declared their unconditional support for Lagu's leadership.[69]

End Notes

1. Collins, *Shadows in the Grass,* pp. 412-3. These safeguards were previously raised in the 'Juba Conference', but the topic was referred to the Governor-General's executive council for study.

2. Daly, *Imperial Sudan,* pp. 241-2.

3. Sam C. Sarkensian. "The Southern Sudan: A Reassessment" *African Studies Review* 16 (1973), pp. 1-22.

4. Collins, *Shadows in the Grass*, pp. 432-35.

5. Ibid., p. 436.

6. Documents on the Sudan, 1899-1953, Egyptian Society of International Law, March 1953, pp. 34-41; Woodward, "Constitutional Development and Independence in the Sudan", pp. 114-120.

7. Collins, *Shadows in the Grass*, p. 442.

8. Ibid., p. 418; I prefer to use the name Workers' Union' rather than Trade Unions, for the later connotes modernity and sophistication.

9. K.D.D.Henderson, *Sudan Republic*, (London: Ernest Benn Limited, 1965) pp. 195-7.

10. Collins, *Shadows in the Grass,* pp. 425-7; Garretson, "The Southern Sudan Welfare Committee and the 1947 Strike in the Southern Sudan" *North East African Studies* 8, 2-3 (1986), pp. 181-91.

11. Collins., p. 426; Garretson, "The Southern Sudan Welfare Committee and the 1947 Strike...", pp. 181-91.

12. Collins., pp. 426.

13. Mohammed O. Bashir, *Tarih al –Harakh al Wataniya Fi al Sudan, 1899-1969* (Dar Al-Sudaniya Lil Kutub, 1980), pp. 248-51.

14. Collins, *Shadow in the Grass*, p. 422 ; Garretson, "The Southern Sudan Wefare Committee and the 1947 Strike ...", pp. 181-91.

15. Collins., p. 423.

16. Daly, *Imperial Sudan*, p. 261.; Garretson, "The Southern Sudan Welfare Committee and ...", pp. 181-91.

17. Collins, *Shadows in the Grass*, p. 439.

18. Ibid., pp. 442-43.

19. Henderson, *The Sudan Republic*, pp. 201-201

20. Collins, *Shadows in the Grass*, P. 449.

21. Samson S. Wassara and Abdel Magid A. Bob, "The Emergence of Organized Political Movement in Southern Sudan 1946-1972" in *The Nationalist Movement in the Sudan,* edited by Mahasin Abdel Gadir Haj a-Safi,(Khartoum: University of Khartoum, 1989), pp. 295-321; Collins, *Shadows in the Grass*, p. 438.

22. Beshir, *Southern Sudan: Background to Conflict,* p. 7.

23. Farouk Akasha Abdun, *Education and Integration in the Sudan:A Historical Review* (Unpublished M. A. Thesis: Beirut, American University of Beirut, 1987), pp. 16-26.

24. Wassara, he Emergence of Organized Political ...", pp. 297-8.

25. Documents on the Sudan, 1899-1956, p. 90.

26. Albino, *Sudan: Southern View point*, pp. 30-2.

27. Oduho, *The Problem of Southern Sudan*, pp. 20-3.

28. Ibid., p. 21.

29. Edgar O'balance, *The Secret War in the Sudan: 1955-1972*, (Conncticut: Archon Books, 1977), p. 36.

30. Collins, *Shadow in the Grass*, p. 445.

31. Ibid,. p. 446.

32. Woodward. "The South in the Sudanese Politics, 1946-1956". pp. 178-92; Collins, *Shadows in the Grass*, p. 446.

33. Beshir Mohammed Said, *The Sudan: Crossroads of Africa*, (London: The Bodley Head, 1965), pp. 72-80.

34. Ducan, *The Sudan: A Record of achievement*, pp. 260-78.

35. Holt, *History of the Sudan*, pp. 159-61.

36. Alier, "The Question of the Southern Sudan", pp. 11-27.

37. Documents on the Sudan, 1899-1956, p. 100.

38. Albino, *Sudan; Southern Viewpoint*, pp. 31-76.

39. Henderson, *Sudan Republic*, p. 202.

40. Collins, *Shadow in the Grass*, p. 448.

41. Ibid., p. 437.

42. Albino, *Sudan: Southern Viewpoint*, pp. 28-35.

43. Cecil Epril, *War and Peace in the Sudan, 1955-1972*, (London: David and Charles, 1974), pp. 19-21.

44. Throughout this chapter the two names, 'Southern Liberal party' and the 'Liberal party' will be use interchangeably, with emphasis on the former name. See Wassara, "The Emergence of the Organized Political ...", p. 298.

45. O'balance, *The Secret War in The Sudan*, pp. 36-8.

46. Oduho, *The Problem of the Southern Sudan*, pp. 24-31. It is difficult to find documents containing the lists of members of the party at this stage. Most of the liberal party leaders were scattered allover the South, hence each has his own files. Those who were in the capital did not have an official office to keep their documents.

47. The Report of the Electoral Commission, (Khartoum December 13, 1953), p. 4.

48. Holt, *History of the Sudan*, pp. 160-61.

49. Documents on the Sudan, 1899-1953, pp. 12-24.

50. Ibid., pp. 11-14.

51. Said, *The Sudan: Crossroads of Africa*, pp. 72-84.

52. Wassara, "The Emergence of Organized Political Leadership ...", p. 299

53. Henderson, *Sudan Republic*, pp. 172-73.

54. The Report of Electral Commission, pp. 12-20; it is reported that during the election campaign the Egyptian media, especially the 'Radio Cairo' had opened six hours program broadcasting in six Southern Sudanese local languaes.

55. Holt, *The History of the Sudan*. p. 161.

56. Daly, *Imperial Sudan*, p. 264.

57. Beshir, *Southern Sudan: Background to Conflict*, p. 72.

58. Collins, *Shadows in the Grass*, p. 454.

59. Report of the Commission of Inquiry on the Disturbances in Southern Sudan, August 1955, Khartoum, October 1956, pp. 107-114.

60. Wassara, "The Emergence of Organized Political ---", p. 301.

61. Collins, Shadows in the Grass, p. 456.

62. Woodward, *The Sudan, 1898-1989:The Unstuble State*, pp. 89 90.

63. Albino, *The Sudan: Southern Viewpoint*, p. 35.

64. Woodward, *The Sudan, 1898-1989*, pp. 90-91; Woodward, "The South in the Sudanese Politics", pp. 178-92.

65. Beshir, *Southern Sudan: Background to Conflict*, p. 73; Gabriel Warburg, *Egypt and Sudan: Studies in History and Politics*, (Frank Cass & Co., 1985), pp. 220-34.

66. Albino, *The Sudan: Southern Viewpoint*, p. 39.

67. Ibid., p. 40.

68. Deng Awour Wenyin, *Southern sudan and the Making of Permanent Constitution in the Sudan*, (Khartoum: University of Juba, 1987), pp. 11-13; also see Oduho, *The Problem of the Southern Sudan*, p. 35; this was the last time the Bloc Members of the parliament participated in the House deliberations before the military coup of November 1958.

69. Wenyin, *Southern sudan and the Making of Permanent ...*, p. 13.

CHAPTER FOUR

Southern Sudan Organizations inside the Sudan

~

SANU Inside

The period between June 1965 and September1969 had witnessed an atmosphere, which could best be described as perpetual internal conflicts in the ranks of Southern political movements both outside and inside the country. In fact, the defection of William Deng Nhial in February 1965 marked the first serious rift within the Southern Sudan Liberation Movement. In the previous chapters we have observed how internal conflicts in the ranks of the Liberal Party and the SANU-in exile weakened these organizations. Competition among political groups within the Southern political fora undermined the effectiveness of these organizations in achieving their goals.

William Deng's SANU was not exception to this situation. William Deng was officially dismissed from SANU mainstream faction in February 1965. Ignoring the decisions taken while away in Europe, in November 1964, William Deng wrote from Geneva to Sirr al-Khatim El-Khalifa, proposing, on behalf of SANU, a round table conference. The content of that letter has already been discussed. The differences between William Deng and his colleagues in SANU were caused by whether the South should federate with North or should the former secede. William Deng chose to take federation with the North, while the SANU hard liners were for secession. On 27th February 1965, William Deng Nhial arrived in Khartoum accompanied by five (5) Southern politicians:[1]

Exekeil Macuai Kodi,

Peter Mow Biet,

Elie Duang Arop,

Rizzigalah Ibrahim

Joseph Bol.

The controversy that ensued around his role before, during and after the round table conference has already been discussed. When the Twelve-Man Committee was formed, William Deng's group got three members including William himself. There was no doubt William Deng's defection to Khartoum shocked many people who knew him as a southern nationalist and a separatist, especially his colleagues in the leadership of the liberation movement. In addition to his role as a founding member of the Southern Sudan liberation movement in exile, William Deng spent most of his time abroad travelling in Europe, the Americans, and Australia explaining the flight of the Southern Sudanese people to the international community. In fact, in order to bring the world's attention to the demand of SANU, William Deng and his colleagues organized in 1963 a series of armed raids into the South from the neighboring countries, hoping that these raids would attract United Nations' involvement. He was a co-author of *The Problem of Southern Sudan* with his colleague, Joseph H. Oduho in summer of 1963. Judging from his activities, William Deng worked more than the rest of Southern politicians to publicize the Southern Sudanese cause.[2]

Apparently, what disappointed William Deng's colleagues was his unexpected change of heart from resolute and a staunch separatist to an advocate of some sort of accommodation with the north, at the very time when militancy seemed to be the only outlet taken unanimously by Southern Sudan liberation movement.

In April 1965, his party was officially registered under the name SANU (inside). On April 9th, 1965, the first SANU-Inside Central Executive Committee was formed. It composed of:[3]

William Deng Nhial,	President
Samuel Aru Bol,	Secretary General
Zakariah Atem,	Deputy Secretary General
P.K. Maboung,	Administrative Secretary
Ezekiel Macuai Kodi,	Secretary for Education
John Amour Kuol,	Culture and Youth
Dr. Tobby Madout Parek,	Spokesman of SANU
Alier Riak Mangere,	President of SANU Youth Organ

Dr. Andrew Wiew Riak,	Member
Permena Kuol,	Member
Alfred Kuol,	Member
Brown Element,	Member
Elie Duang Arop,	Member
Joseph Bol,	Member
Peter Mow Biet,	Member
Rizzigalla I. Mourwell,	SANU Representative, Bahr al-Ghazal
Micha Watta,	SANU Representative, Equatoria
Johathan Malwal Leek,	Chairman SANU Upper Nile

The main objective of the new party was to secure, peacefully, the implementation of the "unanimous" demand accepted by the Sudan parliament on 19th, December 1955 that a federal system of government will be applied to the Sudan.4 It was William Deng SANU opinion that the Sudan's multi-racial character required that it should be governed by a federal system. This explains why his party throughout its existence, stood against a unitary-Islamic Constitution.[5]

Between the 21st April and 8th May 1965 elections were held in the North. The South was exempted from these elections due to the instability there. SANU and Southern Front boycotted these elections and hence were instrumental in the above decision. On 14th June 1965, Mohammed Ahmed Mahjoub formed Umma-NUP coalition government. SANU was allocated two ministerial posts, after the Southern Front turned them down. Andrew Wiew Riak and Alfred Wol were appointed to represent SANU and the third post went to Both

Diu of the revived Liberal Party.[6] However, SANU ministers in the cabinet resigned on the ground that the Liberal Party participation in the cabinet was not necessary since in the view of SANU leadership, the Liberal Party did not have popular support in the South. The two SANU ministers, following their resignation, further defected from SANU and formed what they called 'Big Six Group'. They included Andrew Wiew, Alfred Wol, Jervase Yak, and Three others. The Big Six got its support mainly from Bahr al-Ghazal and Upper Nile Province.[7] The Big Six Group continued to challenge William Deng's power within the party. When on 25th July 1966 Sadiq al-Mahdi formed his coalition government SANU and the Southern Front were not represented.

The new government decided to hold by-election in the remaining Southern (36) constituencies. While the Southern Front announced its boycott, SANU decided to participate. On 8th March 1967, elections were held in the South. SANU got ten (10) seats including William Deng.[9]

Between February 1965 and October 1967, William Deng's main task was to organize his party structures; gain popular support in the North and the South. His oratory and strong personality remained to dominate the party throughout its existence. In an attempt to explain the reasons underlying his unexpected return to Khartoum from exile, he visited several cities in the South discussing all aspects of his programs with community leaders in the South. His controversial tours to East Africa brought conflicts in the Southern leadership in exile. SANU opened branches in the three Southern provinces.

However, its popular base remained in Bahr al-Ghazal. Its headquarters was based in Khartoum, where a youth club, evening school and some other activities were conducted.

In a calculated move to win over the support of young southerners in the capital, SANU established a youth wing, which it called "SANU Youth Organ, SYO." The SYO established in October 1967, a monthly magazine, called *SANU Youth Organ Monthly Bulletin*. It printed its first issue in October 1967. The editorial staff composed of Alier Riak Mangere, L.D. Logoye, G. M. Kok and Alier Monyroor.

By November 1967, differences between the 'Big Six' and William Deng on the one hand, and between him and the Southern Front reached an alarming climax. The 'Big Six' group was challenging the power base of SANU itself-Bahr al-Ghazal. Meanwhile, SANU accused the Southern Front of demanding uncompromising and unattainable request, self-determination, which according to SANU the North will never concede.10 With elections at hand, counter and sometimes, personal accusations between SANU and Southern Front leaders continued unabated. Declaring his party readiness to participate in the forthcoming elections, William Deng informed his supporters through SANU Youth Bulletin in November 1967:

> *"There is much speculation these days whether or not the general elections will be held in February 1968 or at a later date. Whatever the case may be, my advise to all SANU supporters is to prepare and go on preparing for election... This time the*

parliament will last for five years, and it is worth our
efforts to produce not only quantity, but quality of
MPs who will stand the test of making the Southern
Sudan stand on its own feet within the frame of one
Sudan... We are urging the government to imple-
ment the Round Table Conference resolutions,
which give the South Self-rules within the Sudan,
enact and enforce the Amnesty laws and lift the
state of emergency. If these things are done, SANU
would expect all the Southern Sudanese wherever
they are to keep calm and maintain peace."[11]

Based on this policy statement SANU selected its candidate who were to run for elections in the three Southern provinces. In Bahr al-Ghazal, the main challenger to SANU was the 'Big Six Group'. In the other two provinces SANU was challenged by the Southern Front and the Northern parties.

From 18th to 25th April 1968, elections were held throughout the country, in which SANU and the Southern Front participated. SANU received fifteen (15) seats, including William Deng. However, on 5th May 1968, one day before the election results were officially announced, the country was shocked by the news that William Deng Nhial and six of his followers were ambushed and killed on the road from Rumbek to Wau. His death shocked the entire South, including his opponents, who appreciated his positive contribution to the southern cause, especially in its initial stages.

After a week of intentional silence, the government announced over 'Radio Omdurman' that William Deng was killed by 'rebels' and that the government have appointment an investigation team.[12] His supporters however, blamed the government for his death. The nature of William's assassination was horrifying. The nature of his death was best described in July 1968 by Alier Riak, the editor of SANU Youth Bulletin in the following words:

> *"William's head was cut off with part of upper skull probably shot off by a vile bullet or bullets. His SANU shirt taken off; his body rested by a tree, with his head and shirt beside him ...The rest of his colleagues were in rows behind him ...by the time the bodies were covered the only flash that was left was that in the hard part of the limbs."[13]*

Alier's article emphasized the fact that William Deng's party-SANU-won many enemies as well as friends among Southerners; but he refused to admit that the assassination was carried out by Southerners.

Two days later after William Deng assassination, residences of SANU candidates and its youth club in Rumbek were attacked and set on fire by the police. Alfred Wol, the leader of the 'Big Six' who lost his seat to one of William's supporters, was accused but denied any involvement. He and Jervase Yak were in Khartoum when the incident took place. Even the Secretary General of SANU, Samuel Aru Bol, was presumed killed for quite a while, but later reappeared. The investigation team appointed to find the SANU's chief assassins did submit its final report. This report became the government official version, which asserted that William was killed by 'outlaws'.[14]

On 8th June 1968 SANU parliamentarians issued a communiqué in which, among other things, they condemned the incident and urged the government to take the following steps:[15]

The formation of a neutral body headed by a judge to investigate into the assassination of our beloved President Mr. William Deng.

Lifting of the state of emergency in the South and the implementation of the resolutions of the Round Table Conference.

Allocation of a special supplementary budget for the economic development of the South.

Embodiment of the recommendations of the twelve-man committee in the constitution and to implement the system immediately.

The parliamentarians promised to continue to defend the rights of the four million Southerners as long as the Sudan remains an independent democratic Republic. On 23rd June 1968, SANU Secretary General, Samuel Aru Bol sent an appeal to Prime Minister Mahjoub urging him to rectify the security situation in the South. He repeated the demands requested by the SANU parliamentarians and concluded his letter by asking the government to bring before the court the assassins of the SANU leader.[16]

Determined to continue the work of its founder, the SANU Executive Committee called for an emergency convention on 20-21 July 1968 in SANU premises in Khartoum. The convention was attended by the Central Executive Committee

THE IDEA OF SOUTH SUDAN

members and Branch Committee representatives. After lengthy discussions, evaluation and deliberations, the convention passed its resolutions. On internal affairs, the convention, resolved that only through implementations of the December 1955 resolution, Round Table resolutions, and the twelve-man committee recommendations could the problem of Southern Sudan be solved peacefully. It also maintained to work with what it called the 'new forces' among the Northern parties. On foreign policy, the meeting called upon the Sudan government to maintain positive neutrality in respect to the Arab and African disputes. It welcomed the UN efforts to solve the Arab-Israeli conflict peacefully. It called upon OAU to take its responsibilities to solve the Nigerian (Biafra) conflict. The convention elected Mr. Samuel Aru Bol as its new president.[17]

The SANU Central Executive Committee

Samuel Aru Bol,	President
Stephen With Ngunhok,	Vice President
Micha A. Watta,	Vice President
Alier Riak Mangere,	Secretary General
Dr. Tobby Madout Parek,	Deputy Secretary General
Henry Toung Chol,	Treasurer
Ezekeil Macuai Kodi,	Secretary for Education
Alfred Uldo Barjouk,	Legal Secretary
Aldo Ajou Deng,	Secretary for Planning and Resettlement
Lual Diing Wol,	Secretary for Information and Public Relations

Under Secretaries
Ezra Majok Chol,
Alexander Bol Kuan,
Bekedit Kuer Thok,
Fidele Mel;
Mohammed Wedaalah
Luku Logoye

Members

Johathan Malwal Leek,	Chairman of Upper Nile Province
Micha A. Watta:	Chairman of Equatoria Province
Mathew Kot:	Chairman of Bahr al-Ghazal Province

Edward Nyang Kuel,
Philip Akot,
Mathew Dau,
Thomas Tenger,
Kother Aluengi,
Camilio Kuot,
Peter M. Biet,
Anyuonic Mabok,
Kothea Kuany,
Hassan Kur,
Akot Antiak
Samuel Deng Amuk.

The new Executive was sworn in and commenced its work immediately. However, ten months, after William Deng's assassination, were not enough for the new leadership to reorganize and reactivate the demoralized party. On 25th May 1969 a group of progressive military officers waged a military coup and banned all the political parties in the country including SANU.

William Deng was an experienced, pragmatic and a mature political leader and above all he was a good tactician. In fact, the uniqueness of his party lay in that he formed, organized and led a one-community dominated political organization. For the period of his political life inside the country, his party participated in parliamentary fora of the country; his party joined many constitutional committees, presented many working papers to the government, and joined opposition ranks with Northern parties several times. However, his party had difficulties cooperating with the Southern Front. William Deng did not live long enough to witness how his proposed form of 'local autonomy' was granted to the South in February 1972. To his political opponents he compromised some of his principles when he advocated federalism instead of separation and self-determination, however to his supporters he was a Sudanese nationalist.

The Southern Front Party
Historians differ as to when the Southern Front Party was founded. Some maintained that it was a group of Southern civil servants, university students and professionals who

emerged in the capital, three or four months after the popular uprising in October 1964. They took the role of spokesmen of the South inside the country. On that capacity, and considering political vacuum in Southern Sudan after the revolution, they participated in the caretaking government of Sirr al-Katim Khalifa. However, according to the founders of the Front, theirs was a mass organization, which had been active underground during the Abboud military regime.

It was originally also called Southern Professional Front before it adopted. The Front nominated three of its executive members to al-Khalifa's cabinet. They were: Element Mboro Bekobo, for Interior, the first Southerner to hold this post; Hilary Paul Logali, for Works and Ezboni Mondiri Gwanza, for communications. Gwanza was replaced with Gordon Mourtat Mayen in March 1965. The Front nominated Luigi Adwok to represent the South in the Supreme Council (a collective presidency, composed of five members). The Front was officially registered in March 1965. Its Executive Committee composed of:[18]

Gordon Abyei,	President
Darious Beshir,	Vice President
Hilary Logali,	Secretary General
Lubari Ramba,	Member
Isaih Majok,	Member
Natale Olwak,	Member
Abel Alier,	Member

On 23rd March 1965, the Southern Front daily newspaper *The Vigilant* went on print in Khartoum. Its editor was Bona Malwal Ring. The paper remained the mouthpiece of the party-except its interruption for six months when it reported Juba and Wau massacres on 15th July 1965. The most noticeable work of the party was its active and positive participation in the preparation of the Round Table Conference in March 1965. The appointment of al-Khalifa's government and its call for a peaceful solution to the Southern Sudan problem resulted in a mix reaction, suspicion and indifference among Southern leadership in exile. In order to assure the Southern exiles of the government's good intentions, the Southern Front took an initiative to send delegates to East Africa. The task of these delegates was two fold: to explain to the Southern leadership in exile the conditions under which the Front was formed, its program; and the role it anticipates to play in the peace process.[19] The second message was to convince the exiles and acquaint them with changes that had taken place inside the country, and the role these exiles would play, if they chose to participate in that peace process.

The Front Executive decided to send delegates to East Africa and the first delegation left Khartoum in November 1964. It composed of Abel Alier, Lubari Ramba and Darious Beshir. Their mission was to meet politicians and refugees in Kenya, Ethiopia and Uganda. In Nairobi the delegation met Fr. Suturnino Lohure and Joseph H. Oduho in Kampala. Having briefed the two leaders of the changes that were taking place in the country, the SANU leaders expressed to their visitors their fears and suspicions of Northern leadership sincerity for a peaceful solution to the problem of the South. The delegation then went to Addis Ababa where it met with the southern refugees and enlightened them of the new developments in Sudan. Despite their efforts to convince the refugees to return home, Southern Front leaders failed to convince the exiles to remove their fears.[20]

Five days after their arrival, Clement Mboro was scheduled to return to Khartoum on December 6th, 1964 after ten days tour to the South. On the appointed date, the Southern Front supporters and other Southern inhabitants of the capital went to the airport to wait and welcome him. Mboro's plane did not arrive on appointed time disappointed with improper explanation given by the airport officials the crowd suspected that misfortune might have happened to him. Riots broke out a lot of property was damaged in the airport. Northerners were attacked randomly. Northerners responded by attacking any southerner (blacks) wherever they were found. Fighting expanded into the three districts (Khartoum, Khartoum North and Omdurman).

On the 7th December, the security authorities gathered Southerners in Omdurman and Khartoum football stadiums for one week. Many Southerners were killed and others were injured. Few days later mass exodus of Southerners from Khartoum and other Northern cities to the South followed. The reaction of Southern front leaders during the incident had shown beyond doubt the popularity of the Front among Southerners in the North and the potential threat its supporters pose particularly in the capital. Later on young Southerners were transported to the South, most of whom joined the ranks of the AnyaNya movement in the bushes of Southern Sudan.[21]

The second delegation of Southern Front to East Africa was led by Abdin Ismail and Ezbon Mondiri. They left Khartoum in January 1965. In Kampala, the delegation concluded an agreement with Ugandan authorities, in which the Ugandan government would help the Sudanese authorities in repatriation and resettlement of Sudanese (Southerners) refugees residing in Uganda. The main objective of the delegation was to win over the neighboring countries and to urge them to pressurize the Southern exiles in their countries to accept the government peace proposal to accept peace proposal and return home.[22]

The third mission of the Front to East Africa composed of Daud Abdellatif, Mou Giir and Akech Mohammed. Their mission was to meet William Deng in Zaire, where he was residing. The delegation was specifically instructed to convince William Deng, whose letter to the Prime Minister had shown a conciliatory gesture, to return home. The Southern Front was aware of divisions among the SANU leaders, especially between Aggrey Jaden and William Deng, hence it acted in such a way, which would make it (the Front) the most effective Southern party in the peace talks. A divided SANU was better than a united one, which might deprive the Front the privilege of Southern Sudan spokesman inside the country. Another method, which the front employed was to send its delegates to particular groups. Delegates to William Deng composed of Dinka members, while those to Aggrey Jaden group were from Equatoria. This was very important and effective approach since Dinka-Equatoria quarrels were instrumental in ineffectiveness of the Southern liberation movement in exile. William

Deng was convinced to return to Khartoum, which he did in February 1965.[23]

The fourth Southern Front delegation to Kampala was led by Hillary Paul Logali. His mission was to convince the hard-liners of SANU into accepting the venue of and participation in the conference. The delegation reminded Aggrey Jaden group that if they refuse to attend, the government was ready to accept William Deng as the sole representative of SANU. Aggrey Jaden faction had no choice but to submit to the Front's blackmailing offer and accepted to attend the conference in Khartoum. The conference was held as discussed earlier, and the Southern Front cooperated closely with Jaden's faction. The following are excerpts from the Southern Front speech in which its objective was clearly stated before the conference:

> *"The relationship which exists between the North and South has been imposed by external body. The wishes and aspirations of the inhabitants of the South have not been considered. What is more, this relationship has been strained by action of Northern governments and Northern individuals and groups with influence...that it requires a reexamination by the Southern Sudanese alone. Hence in response to the facts of history and the Northern argument that Southerners wanted unity and that only a hand-ful adventurers wished to disturb the status quo, the South should be allowed to decide its destiny through the free exercise of self-determination."*[24]

Few months after the Round Table Conference the new
Southern Front Executive Committee was elected with key
positions distributed as follows:

Clement Mboro Bekobo,   President
Gordon Mourtat Mayen,   Vice President
Hilary Paul Logali,   Secretary General

The following members were also elected:
Gordon Abyei,
Darious Beshir,
Lubari Ramba,
Isaih Majok,
Abel Alier Kuay,
Natale Olwak,
Ambrose Ring,
Luigi Adwok,
Ezboni Mondiri,
Abdin Ismail,
Daud Abdel Latif,
Mow Giir,
Akech Mohamed,
Bona Malwal Ring,
Othwanh Dak,
Othwonh Bougho,
Romano Hassan,
Henry Bugho
Bhan Malwal.[25]

Meanwhile, with the Round Table Conference behind, the Northern parties began preparations for national elections. It is to be recalled that the Front was not a partner to the 'National Charter', a document, which all the Northern parties signed after the October 1964 revolution. In that Charter a definite date for general elections was fixed. The Front argued that the Charter was exclusively a Northern-negotiated hence the Front was not bound by its provisions. In a memorandum to the Prime Minister, the Front leadership demanded among other things, the following to be carried out, if it has to participate in the forthcoming elections:[26]

That Northern political parties should take clear steps toward the solution of the problem. i.e. implementation of the Round Table Conference resolutions not later than second week of June 1965.

The South should be represented in the government on the basis of population ratio.

Southern Sudan members in the cabinet be nominated by the South and appointed by the Prime Minister.

That the parliament elected on April 21st, 1965 in the North, should not sit until the Southern problem was solved or at least until such a time when the South decided to elect its own representatives to parliament.

It should be the policy of the government that elections would not take place directly or indirectly in the Southern region on April 21st, 1965.

Despite Southern opposition to the elections, the Northern parties went ahead preparing for the elections. Elections were eventually held in the North on April 21st. However, the government had not kept its promise regarding exclusion of the South in these elections. Some Northern traders in the South claimed that they had been elected unopposed and appealed to the Supreme Court that declared them as duly elected to the Constituent Assembly. Both SANU and Southern Front protested against the court decision, but their protestations were not considered.[27]

Having boycotted the elections, the Southern Front was shocked by two dramatic incidents, which took place in the South. The Front leadership was convinced that the two incidents, in Juba and Wau, were directed against its followers. The two incidents led to the death of 473 Southerners.

On 9th July 1965, a dramatic incident was started by an argument over a transistor radio between an army sergeant and a Southern nurse at Juba hospital. As a result of disagreement, a physical fight started and the Sergeant received injuries. The news of the fight reached the Northern soldiers who were returning from cinema at 10 p.m. They rushed to their headquarters, took their guns and started burning and shooting. In the morning over 3,000 grass-houses had been burned and over 400 people dead.

In Wau the shooting incident was limited but horrifying. On 11th July 1965, Ottavio Deng and his cousin Cypriano Cier were married in Wau Cathedral to two sisters, daughters of chief Benjamin Lang. Witnesses in the reception reported that a Northern soldier entered the house and asked four Northerners who were participating in the ceremony to leave.

Few minutes later, the guests discovered that the house of the reception was surrounded by the army, who without warning opened fired and killed 76 people instantly. The newly wed couples were among the murdered people at the reception.

The Southern Front leadership insisted that the two incidents were intended to eliminate its members who formed the civil servant cadre in these cities.[28] The Front's paper, *Vilgilant'* reported angrily the two incidents. The editor, Bona Malwal and the proprietor of the paper, Darious Beshir, were taken to court on the ground that they reported false information. The paper was stopped for six months. The two men were acquitted from the charges after the lawyer of the paper, Abel Alier Kuay, produced witnesses among them was a certain James Yol.[29]

On 25th June 1966, the twelve-man committee completed its recommendations. Southern Front had played an active role in this committee. In September the committee submitted its recommendations to the government of Sadiq al-Mahdi. The Prime Minister appointed two civil servants. Arop Yor Ayik and Jervase Yak to represent the South in his cabinet. Instead of reconvening Round Table Conference, as recommended by the Twelve-man Committee, the Prime Minister convened an All-Party Conference in October 1966. In this conference, the South was allocated seven members: SANU-two; Southern Front two, and one each for the Sudan Unity Party, the Liberal Party and the Sudan Peace Party. The Southern Front boycotted that conference.[30]

When the government decided to hold by-elections in the South on 8th March 1967, the Southern Front maintained its previous position and boycotted it. On 16th May 1967 Mohammed Ahmed Mahjoub formed his coalition government. He chose to cooperate with the Southern Front, having argued that SANU was loosing support in Upper Nile and Equatoria.[31] The new government appointed Both Diu of the Liberal Party, Hilary Paul Logali of the Southern Front and Alfred Wol of SANU to the cabinet. Philemon Majok of the Sudan Unity Party represented the South in the Supreme Council.[32] When differences among the coalition partners in the government reached uncompromising stage, it was decided that general elections would be held in April 1968.

Confronted with potential isolation in the capital on the one hand, and the fear that its supporters in the South might join SANU, Southern Front decided to contest the 1968 elections. It was not definitely an easy decision. The party leadership believed that the presence of the Front in parliament would prevent adoption of a constitution, which may ignore the Southern demands. However, by accepting to contest the elections, the Southern Front lost face in the South, since their participation meant the reversion of their previous position that the situation in the South was not conductive for a free and peaceful election. The security situation was not back to normal, and the state of emergency imposed since August 1955 was not lifted. The Southern Front participation in April 1968 elections was considered by some of its supporters as hypocritical.[33]

Elections were eventually held throughout the country from 18th to 25th April 1968. Out of 60 seats allocated to the South, the Front got 10 seats; 4 candidates contested as independents, including Luigi Adowk, who was dismissed from the Front a year earlier. In late May 1968, Prime Minister Mahjoub formed DUP-Umma (pro-Imam Hadi) – Southern Front Coalition government. Clement Mboro and Hilary Paul Logali were appointed ministers of Mines and Industry, Labour and Social Services respectively. Jervase Yak succeeded Philemon Majok on the Supreme Council.[34]

Throughout its existence, the Front leadership tried to hard to hide its separatist image. In fact, it maintained that it had no control over AnyaNya, but never offer apology for AnyaNya's actions. By 1967 some Southern Front members either left the party or left the country. In fact, two prominent Front Executive Committee members went to exile in East Africa. They were Gordon Mourtat and Ezbon Mondiri who became active members in exile and held prominent positions.[35]

Since its creation, the Southern Front was considered to be the radical Southern party inside the country. In fact, the Front was the principal target of all Northern political parties. In 1967, the Front developed what might be called 'working relationship' with the DUP and the Imam Hadi's wing of Umma party.[36] The Front had participated in all constitutional committees in the country. In December 1968, for example, a final draft of what turned out to be a unitary Islamic Constitution was presented to the Assembly. The Southern members of the Constitutional Committee walked out in a protest of the draft. The Southern spokesman told the Assembly that the draft proposed, if promulgated as the national constitution, it would discriminate Southerners on the ground of religion and race, hence it was not acceptable to the South.[37]

Frustrated by continuous rivalry among the Northern parties, the Southern Front faced difficulties to push through its vision of self-determination nor was it able to reach some sort of accommodation, which would give the South a special status within the united Sudan. It was Southern Front leadership belief that without a strong and united Southern leadership inside the country, the Northern governments would get a chance to build up puppet leaders for the South.

By and large, the Southern Front and SANU were most of the time fighting each other, more than the Northern parties. Their two newspapers, *Vigilant* and *SANU Youth Bulletin*, sharply accused each other of being an agent to the government. An illustrative example of these counter accusations would be the following excerpts from an article written in SANU Youth Bulletin in February 1967:

"The statement made by Andrew Wiew, (one of the Big Six Group) published in the paper, *Vigilant*, is opportunistic in that its aims are like that of *Vigilant* to win the sympathy from the government problems and particularly that of the South... Mr. Wiew's attack on SANU President can best be described as being mere and a pathetic narrow selfish interest to use the time of confusion in order to collect some sympathetic look from the Pan-Arabists who are afraid of regional system of government in the Sudan, to use *Vigilant* and some blind Sudanese to prevent the political awakening of the true sons of the Sudanese people in the regions like Western, Eastern and the Southern Sudanese".[38]

In the morning hours of 25th May 1969, the military, led by Colonel Jaafar Mohmed Nimeiri, waged a successful blood-less coup. The Southern Front, like other Sudanese political parties, was dissolved. However, with the new rulers desper-ately in need of Southern Sudan backup, the Southern Front leadership assumed the role of Southern representative, this time under new name – 'Southern Intellectuals'. On that capacity they negotiated peace settlement with the Southern Sudan Liberation Movement (SSLM) under General Joseph Lagu Yanga in February 1972.

Abel Alier Kuay, Chairman of the government delegation to the peace talks was appointed in April 1972, Vice President of the Republic and the first President of the High Executive Council, the Southern Sudan regional government. With Southern Front officially in control of the South, SANU and the Southern Front rivalry resurfaced.

The Southern regional government became the new theatre of that rivalry. Front prominent figures such as Bonal Malwal Ring, Henry Buogho, Romano Hassan, Joshua Dei Wal, Hilary Paul Logali, Peter Gatkuoth Gual, and a few others occupied high positions in the government. Likewise, SANU leaders participated in the regional government; leaders such as late Samuel Aru Bol, Dr. Tobby Madout Parek, Ezekeal Macuai Kodi, and others joined the regional government. As the Regional Government developed into a stable authority, SANU partisans, such as Aldo Ajou Deng, Tobby Madout and Simon

Mawia, openly opposed what they called 'Southern Front hegemony'. Had the Southern Front achieved its main objectives? To some it did, but to most of its leaders it did not, for the local autonomy granted to the South in February 1972 was a compromise and not a final solution to the 'Southern Sudan Problem'.

End Notes

1. Alier, *Southern, pp. 28-40.*
2. Epril, *War and Peace in the Sudan*, p. 63.
3. Nyquist, "The Sudan; Prelude to the Elections", pp.263-273.
4. Beshir, *Southern Sudan ---*, p. 94.
5. O'Balance, *The Secret War in the Sudan*
6. Mahjoub, *Democracy on the Trial*, pp. 75-77.
7. Albino: *The Sudan: Southern Viewpoint*, pp. 63-67.
8. Ibid., p. 66.
9. P.K. Mboung, "Southern Leaders remember the South", *SANU Youth Monthly Bulletin*, 2 (November 1967), p. 16-19.
10. "President of SANU, Mr. William Deng on the Coming Elections", *SANU Youth Monthly Bulletin*, 2 (November 1967), p. 1.
11. O'Balance, *The Secret War in the Sudan*, p. 100.
12. Aliar Riak, The Public Reactions on the Assassination of the SANU President, William Deng *SANU Youth Organ Monthly Bulletin* 8 (July 1968), pp. 16-19.
13. Albino, *The Sudan; Southern Viewpoint*, p. 74.
14. "SANU Appeals to Mahjoub's Government to Rectify the Choatic Situation in the South", *SANU Youth Organ Monthly Bulletin* 8 (1968), pp. 5-8.
15. Ibid., p. 8.
16. SANU Appeals....,pp. 5-8.
17. Ibid., 8
18. Wai, *African-Arab* Conflict in the Sudan, pp. 98-105.
19. Beshir, *Southern Sudan: Background to Conflict*, pp. 99-107.
20. O'Balance, *The Secret War in the Sudan*, pp. 68-78.
21. Alier, *Southern Sudan*, pp. 24-26.
22. Ibid, pp. 27-29.
23. Ibid., p. 28.
24. B. S. Sharma, he 1965 Elections in the Sudan", *The Political Quarterly* 37, 4 (1966), pp. 441-52.

25. Alier, *Southern Sudan ---*, p. 26; Wai, *African Arab Conflict in the Sudan*, p. 100.

26. Sharma, he 1965 elections in the Sudan", pp. 441-52.

27. Albino, *The Sudan: Southern Viewpoint*, pp. 64-66; Alier, *Southern Sudan*, pp. 36-40.

28. Albino, *The Sudan ---*, p. 66.

29. O'Balance, *The Secret War in the Sudan*, pp. 95-101

30. Albino, *The Sudan: Southern Viewpoint*, pp. 72-75.

31. O'Balance, *The Secret War ---*, p. 100; Shaffer, "The Sudan: Arab-African Confrontation", pp. 142-6/178.

32. Howell, "Politics in the Southern Sudan", pp. 163-178.

33. Charles Gurdon, *Sudan at the Crossroad* (Kent; The Middle East and North African Studies Press, 1984), pp. 14-19.

34. Alier, *Southern Sudan*, p. 40.

35. Albino, *The Sudan: Southern Viewpoint*, p. 76.

36. "Andrew Wiew Advocates the Union of the South With Egypt" *SANU Youth Organ Monthly Bulletin* 5 (February 1968), p. 15.

37. Alier, *Southern Sudan*, pp. 124-192. In these pages, Alier discusses, implicitly the SANU-AnyaNya Southern Front rivalry behind the scenes. Although he avoids naming partisanship of the groups involved, he admits that they were existed opposition to his presidency of the High Executive Council of the South, 1972-1978.

38. Alier, *Southern Sudan*, pp. 124-192

References in English

Books and biographies

Ahmed, H. M. Mohamed. *Sudan: The Christian Design, a Study of the Missionary Factor in the Sudan's Cultural and Political Integration, 1843-1986.* Leicester: Islamic Foundation, 1989.

Ajawin, Lam Akol. *SPLM/SPLA: Inside an African Revolution.* Khartoum: Khartoum University Press, 2001.

Ali, Taisier M., and Robert O. Matthews, eds. *Civil War and Failed Efforts for Peace in the Sudan.* McGill Queen's University Press, 1999.

Beaton, A. C.*Equatoria Province Handbook. Vol. 2: 1936-1948.* Khartoum, n. p., 1949.

Beshir, Mohamed Omer. *The Southern Sudan. From Conflict to Peace.* London: Chrisptopher Hurst, 1975.

_____, *Tarih al –Harakh al Wataniya Fi al Sudan, 1899-1969* (Dar Al-Sudaniya Lil Kutub, 1980), pp. 248-51

_____, ed. *Southern Sudan: Regionalism and Religion.* Khartoum: Khartoum University Press, 1984.

Beshir, Zakaria. *Islamic Movement in the Sudan: Issues and Challenges.* Leicester: Islamic Foundation, 1987.

Betts, Tristram. *The Southern Sudan: The Cease-Fire and After.* London: The Africa Publications Trust, 1974.

Both, Peter Lam. *South Sudan: Forgotten Tragedy.* Calgary: University of Calgary Printing Services, 2002.

Churchil, Winston Leonard Spencer. *The River War, and Historical Account of the Reconquest of the Sudan.* London: Longmans & Co., 1899.

Collins, Robert O. *King Leopold and the Upper Nile, 1899-1909.* New Haven: Yale University Press, 1968.

_____. *The Southern Sudan in Historical Perspective.* Transaction Publishers, 2006.

Crabites, Pierre. *Gordon, the Sudan and Slavery.* London: Routledge and Sons, Ltd., 1933.

_____. *The Winning of the Sudan.* London: George Routledge and Sons, Ltd., 1934.

Daly, Martin W., and Ahmed A. Sikainga, eds. *The Civil War in the Sudan.* London: British Academic Press, 1993.

Deng, Francis M. *Dynamics of Identification: A Basis for National Integration in the Sudan*. Khartoum: University of Khartoum Press, 1974.

_____. *War of Visions: Conflict of Identities in the Sudan*. Washington, DC: Brooking Institution, 1995.

Deng, Francis Mading and Prosser Gifford, eds. *Search for Peace and Unity in the Sudan*. Washington, DC: Wilson Center Press, 1987.

Diop, Chieka Anta. *Precolonial Black Africa A Comparative Study of the Political and Social Systems of Europe and Blackafrica*. Lawrence Hill, 1987.

_____. *The African Origin of Civilization Myth or Reality*. Lawrence Hill, *1989.*

_____. *Civilization or Barbarism An Authentic Anthropology*. Lawrence Hill, *1991.*

_____. *The Peopling of Ancient Egypt the Deciphering of the Meroitic Script*. Karmak House Pub, *1997.*

_____. *Towards the African Renaissance Essays in African Culture and Development 1946-1960,* Red Sea Press, 2000.

Documents on the Sudan, 1899-1953. Cairo: Egyptian Society of International Law, March 1953, pp. 34-41.

Eprile, Cecil, *War and Peace in the Sudan, 1955-1972* (London: David and Charles, 1974), pp. 19-21.

Evans-Pritchard, Sir Edward E. *Administrative Problems in Southern Sudan*. Oxford: Clarendon Press, 1938.

Fluehr-Lobban, C, Richard A. Lobban, and John O. Voll. *Historical Dictionary of the Sudan*. 2d ed. Metuchen, NJ: Scarecrow Press, 1992.

Gordon, Charles. *Equatoria Under Egyptian Rule*. Cairo: Cairo University Press, 1963.

Gray, Richard. *A History of the Southern Sudan, 1839-1889*. London: Oxford University Press, 1961.

Greene, Thomas H, *Comparative Revolutionary Movements* (NJ: Prentice-Hall, Inc., 1990), pp. 88-103.

Gurdon, Charles , *Sudan at the Crossroad* (Kent: The Middle East and North African Studies Press, 1984), pp. 14-19.

Hamilton, John A., ed. *The Anglo-Egyptian Sudan from Within*. Foreword by Lt. Colonel Sir Stewart Symes. London: Faber & Faber, Ltd., 1935.

Harir, Sherif, and Terje Tvedt. *Short-Cut to Decay: The Case of the Sudan*. Uppsala: Nordoska Africainstitute, 1994.

Hassan, Yusuf . *Arabs and the Sudan: From Seventh to the Early Sixteenth Century*. Edinburgh: Edinburgh University Press, 1967.

Henderson, K.D.D., *Sudan Republic* (London: Ernest Been Limited, 1965), pp. 160, 195-97.

Hunwick, John O., ed. *Religion and National Integration in Africa: Islam, Christianity, and Politics in the Sudan and Nigeria*. Evanston, IL: Northwestern University Press, 1992.

Hill, Richard L. *A Biographical Dictionary of the Sudan*. 2d ed. London: Frank Cass, 1967.

Hutchison, Sharon. H. *Nuer Dilemmas: Coping with Money, War and State*. Berkeley: University of California Press, 1996.

Johnson, Douglas H. *The Southern Sudan*. London: London: Minority Rights Group, 1988.

_____. *The Root Causes of Sudan's Civil War*. Lawrenceville, NJ: Africa World Press, 1999.

Khalid, Mansour. *Numeiri and the Revolution of Dismay*. London: Kegan Paul International, 1985.

_____. *The Government They Deserve: The Role of the Elite in Sudan's Political Evolution*. London: Kegan Paul International, 1990.

Kirk-Greene, A.H. *The Sudan Political Service: A Preliminary Profile*. Oxford: Oxford University Press, 1982.

Kok, Peter Nyot. *A Pilgrimage in the Middle Ages: Nimeiri's Sharia in the Sudan*. Hambourg: Maz Planck Institute, 1990.

_____. *Governance and Conflict in the Sudan, 1985-1995: Analysis and Documentation*. Hambourg: Deutsch Orient Institut, 1996.

Lako, George Tomb. *Southern Sudan: The Foundations of the War Economy*. Wien, 1993.

Lesch, Ann Mosley. *Sudan : Contested National Identities*. Oxford : James Currey, 1999.

Levin, Deborah, ed. *The Condominium Remembered : The Making of the Sudanese State*. Vol. 1. Durham : University of Durham Press, 1991.

Llyong, Taban lo. *Eating Chiefs : Lwo Culture from Lolwe to Malakal*. London : Heinmann Educational, 1970.

_____. *Popular Culture of East Africa : Oral Literature*. Nairobi : Longman, 1972.

_____. *Another Last Word*. Nairobi : Heinmann Kenya, 1990.

_____, ed. *Women in Folktales and Short Stories of Africa*. Pietersburg : Azalea, 1997.

de Mabior, John Garang. *The Call for Democracy in the Sudan*. London: Kegan Paul International, 1992.

_____. *The Vision of New Sudan: Questions of Unity and Identity*. Cairo: Consortium for Policy Analysis and Development Strategies (COPADES), 1998

Mack, John. Ed. *Culture and History in the Southern Sudan: Archaeology, Linguistics and Ethnology*. Nairobi: Institute of East Africa, 1984.

Madour, El-Mahdi. *A Short History of Sudan*. Oxford: Oxford University Press, 1965.

Mahgoub, Mohamed Ahmed. *Democracy on Trial: Reflections on Arab and African Politics*. London: Andre Deutsch Limited, 1974.

Mahmuod, Fatima Babiker, ed. *Calamity in the Sudan: Civilian versus Military Rule*. London: Institute for African Alternatives, 1988.

Malwal, Bona. *Cultural Diversity and National Unity*, Cairo, 1976.

_____. *The Sudan: A Second Challenge to Nationhood*, London: New York: Thornton Books, 1985.

Mawut, Lazarus Leek. *Dinka Resistance to Condominium Rule, 1902-1932*. London: Ithaca Press, 1983.

Newbold, Sir Douglas. *The Making of the Modern Sudan, the Life and Letters of Sir Douglas Newbold of the Sudan Political Service*. London: Faber and Faber, 1953.

Nyaba, Peter Adwok. *Politics of Liberation in South Sudan: An Insider's View*. Kampala: Fountain Publishers, Ltd., 1997.

O'Balance, Edgar, *The Secret War in the Sudan: 1955-1972*, (Conncticut: Archon Books, 1977), p. 36.

Oduho, Joseph and William Deng, *The Problem of Southern Sudan*, (London: Oxford University press, 1963), pp. 13-20.

O'Fahey, R. S. *Southern Sudan: Symposium of Conflicts in the Middle African Region*. London: International Institute of Strategic Studies, 1971.

Ogot, B.A. *History of the Southern Luo*. Vol. 1: Migration and Settlement. 1967.

Prunnier, Gerard. *From Peace to War: The Southern Sudan, 1972-1984*. Hull University Press, 1986.

Report of the Commission of Inquiry on the Disturbances in Southern Sudan, August 1955, Khartoum, October 1956, pp. 107-114.

Ruay, Deng D. Akol. *The Politics of Two Sudans.* Uppsala: Nordiska Afrikainstitute, 1994.

Al-Safi, Mohasin Hag, ed. *The Nationalist Movement in the Sudan.* Khartoum: Khartoum University Press, 1989.

Said, Beshir Mohammed, *The Sudan: Crossroads of Africa,* (London: The Bodley Head, 1965), pp. 72-80.

Sanderson, Lilian P. and Neville Sanderson, *Education, Religion and Politics in Southern Sudan, 1899-1964* (London: Ithaca Press, 1981), pp. 81-95.

Santandrea, Stefano. *A Tribal History of Western Bahr El Ghazal.* Bologna: Edirica Nigrizia, 1964.

Seligman, G. G., and B. Z. Seligman. *Pagan Tribes of the Nilotic Sudan.* London, 1932.

Shibeika, Mekki. *British Policy in the Sudan: 1882-1902.* London: Oxford University Press, 1952.

_____. *Independent Sudan.* New York: Spelter, 1959.

Sidahamed, Abdel Salam. *Politics and Islam in Contemporary Sudan.* New York: St. Martin's Press, 1997.

Spaulding, Jay and Stephenie Beswick, eds. *White Nile Black Blood War, Leadership and Ethnicity from Khartoum to Kampala.* Lawrenceville, NJ: Red Sea Press, 2000.

Theobald, Alan Buchan. *The Mahdiyya: A History of the Anglo-Egyptian Sudan, 1881-1899.* London: Longmans, 1951.

Voll, John O. The Political Impact of Islam in the Sudan: Numayri's Islamization Program. Washington, DC: Department of State, 1984. .

Wai, Dustan M., ed., *African-Arab Conflict in the Sudan* (New York; African Publishing Company, 1981), p. 75.

Warburg, Gabriel R, *Egypt and Sudan: Studies in History and Politics,* (Frank Cass & Co., 1985), pp. 220-34

_____. *Historical Discord in the Nile Valley.* Evanston, IL: Northwestern University Press, 1992.

_____. *Islam, Sectarianism and Politics in Sudan since the Mahdiyya.* London: C. Hurst & Co., 2002.

.Wenyin, Deng Awour, *Southern sudan and the Making of Permanent Constitution in the Sudan* (Khartoum: University of Juba, 1987), pp. 11-13.

Yangu, Alexis Mbali. *The Nile Turn Red.* New York: Pageant Press Inc., 1966.

Yoh, John G Nyuot. *Christianity in the Sudan: An Annotated Bibliography.* Amman, Royal Institute for Inter-Faith Studies, 1999.

2. Periodicals

Abdel Salam, AlFatih, "Ethnic Politics in the Sudan" In *Ethnicity, Conflict and National Integration in the Sudan*, edited by Sayyid H. Hurreiz (Khartoum: University of Khartoum Press, 1989), pp. 29-68.

Abdel Wahab O. El-Affendi, "Discovering the South Sudanese Dilemma for Islam in Africa." *African Affairs* 89 (July 1990) : 371-389.

Alier, Abel, "The Southern Sudan Question" In *The Southern Sudan and the Problem of National Integration*, edited by Dustan M. Wai (London: Frank Cass, 1973), pp. 9-27.

"Andrew Wiew Advocates the Union of the South with Egypt" *SANU Youth Organ Monthly Bulletin* 5 (February 1968), p. 15.

Badal, R.K., "The Rise and Fall of Separatism in Southern Sudan" *African Affairs* 75 (1976), pp. 463-74.

Bechtold, Peter K., "Military Rule in the Sudan: The first Five Years of Jaafar Numayri" *The Middle East Journal, 29 (1975)* pp. 16-32.

Browbent, P. B. "Sudanese Self-Government." *International Affairs* 30 (1954) : 320-330.

Bure, B. Yongo. "The Underdevelopment of Southern Sudan Since Independence." In *Civil War in the Sudan*, edited by M. W. Daly and Ahmad S. Sikainga, 51-77. London: British Academic Press, 1993.

de Chand, David. "The Sudan's Civil War: Is a Negotiation Solution Possible?" *Africa Today* 36, nos. 3-4 (1989) : 55-63.

Deng, Francis M., "The Identity Factor in the Sudanese Conflict" In *Conflict and Peacemaking in Multiethnic Societies,* edited by Joseph V. Montville (Toronto: Lexington Books, 1991), pp. 343-362.

"District Commissioner Rumbek's Reaction to 1946 Southern Policy, Rumbek, January 29, 1947" In Beshir's *Southern Sudan Background to Conflict*, pp. 130-31.

" Further Reactions to 1946 Southern Policy, Wau, March 10, 1947" In Beshir's *Southern Sudan: Background to Conflict*, pp.134-43.

Garang, Joseph Ukel. "On Economics and Regional Autonomy." In *The Southern Sudan: The Problem of National Integration*, edited by Dustan M. Wai, 83-92. London: Frank Cass, 1973.

Garretson, P., "The Southern Sudan Welfare Committee and the 1947 Strike in the Southern Sudan" *North East African Studies* 8, nos. 2-3 (1986), pp. 181-91.

Gatkuoth, James Mabor. "Ethnicity and Nationalism in the Sudan." Ecumenical Review 47, no. 2 (1995) : 206-216.

Ghaboush, Philip Abbas and others. "A Proposed Solution to the Arab Problem in Sudan." *Midstream* 17 (November 1971) : 59-63.

"Governor Equatoria Reacts to Southern Policy of 1946, Juba, December 23, 1946" In Beshir's *Southern Sudan: Background to Conflict*, pp.122-23.

Great Britain, Parliament, *Sessional Papers* (House of Commons) "Report on Administration of the Sudan for the Year 1948", 1950-51, CMD. 8181 Vol. XIX, p.817.

Grundes, Kenneth W., "Nationalism and Separatism in East Africa" *Africa* (February 1968), pp. 90-94/112.

Gwado-Ayoker, Kunijok. "Interpreting the South." In *Sudan since Independence*, edited by Peter Woodward et al., , 152-160. Aldershot: Gower Press, 1986.

Hamid, Mohammad Beshir. "Devolution and National Integration in the Southern Sudan." In *Sudan since Independence*, edited by Peter Woodward et al., 121-142. Aldershot: Gower Press, 1986.

Hassan, Yusuf Fadil, "The Sudanese Revolution of October 1964" *The Journal of Modern African Studies*, 5, 4 (December 1967), pp. 491-510.

Heradides, Alexis, "Secessionist Minorities and external involvement" *International Organization* 44, 3 (1990), pp. 341-378.

Hill, R., "Government and Christian Missions in the Anglo-Egyptian Sudan, 1899-1914" *Middle Eastern Studies*, 1 (January 1965), pp. 113-34.

Hurreiz, Sayid H. "Ethnic, Cultural and National Identity in the Sudan: An Overview." In *Ethnicity, Conflict and National Integration in the Sudan*, edited by Sayid H. Hureiz and El-Fatih A. Abdel Salam, 69-101. Khartoum: University of Khartoum Press, 1989.

Jal, Gariel Giet. "The Anglo-Egyptian Occupation of the Sobat and Pipor Valleys, 1898-1911." *Second International Sudan Studies Conference Papers*. Durham: University of Durham, 1991.

Johnson, Douglas H. "Tribal Boundaries and Border Wars: Nuer-Dinka Relations in Upper Nile Province, c. 1860-1976." A paper presented at the Twenty-Third annual meeting of the African Studies Association, Philadelphia, 1980.

Kasfir, Nelson, "Southern Sudanese politics since the Addis Ababa Agreement" *African Affairs* 76 (April 1977), pp. 143-166.

Khalid, Mansour. "Ethnic Integration in the Sudan." *Review of International Affairs* 24, no. 54 (5February 1973) : 22-26.

_____. "Sudan: A Plea for Pluralism; Northern Politicians Must Share Responsibility for Sudan's Current Political Crises." *Africa Report* 30 (July 1985) :53-57.

El-Khawas, Mohamed A. "The Problem of Southern Sudan." *African Studies Review* (Cairo) 4 (1975) :21-41.

Kyle, Keith, "The Southern Problem in the Sudan" *The World Today* 22 (1966), pp. 512-20.

_____, "The Sudan Today" *African Affairs* 65 (1966), pp. 233-44.

Lagu, Joseph. " "Southerners' View of the Sudan Settlement." *New Middle East* 49 (1972) : 17-18.

_____, "Dynamics of Cooperation between the AnyaNya and the People" *Grass Curtain*, 1, 4 (1971), pp. 5-6.

Lesch, Ann Mosley. "Confrontation in the Southern Sudan." *Middle East Journal* 40 (1986) : 410-28.

Lohure, Saturnino. "Southern Sudan: Why the Talks Broke Down." *Reporter* (Nairobi) 9 (April 1965).

Loiria, Anglo Lobale, "The Juba Conference: A Critical Appraisal" In *The Nationalist Movements in the Sudan,* edited by Mahasin Abdel Sadir Haj al-Safi (Khartoum: University of Khartoum press `989), pp. 266-94.

Mazrui Ali Amin. "Religion and Democracy in the Republic of the Sudan." *Makerere Journal* 11 (1965) : 39-50.

Mboung, P.K., "Southern Leaders remember the South" *SANU Youth Monthly Bulletin*, 2 (November 1967), p. 16-19.

"1930 Memorandum on the Southern policy" In Beshir's *Southern Sudan: Background to Conflict*, pp. 115-18; Henderson, *Sudan Republic*, pp. 161-66.

"1946 Memorandum on Southern policy, Khartoum, December 1946" In Mohammad *O. Beshir's Southern Sudan: Background to Conflict*, pp. 119-21.

Musa, Omer El Haq, "Reconciliation, Rehabilitation and Development Efforts in Southern Sudan," *The Middle East Journal*, (Winter (1973), pp. 1-6.

An Naim, Abdullahi Ahmed. "Constitutional Discourse and the Civil War in the Sudan." In *Civil War in the Sudan*, edited by M. W. Daly and Ahmed A. Sikainga, 97-116. London: British Academic Press, 1993.

Niblock, Timothy C., "A New political system in the Sudan" *Affrican Affairs* 73, (October 1974), pp. 408-418.

Nyquist, Thomas E., "The Sudan; Prelude to Elections" *Middle East Journal*, 19, 3 (1965) pp. 263-72.

Orlebar, J. H. R. "The Story of the Sudan Defense Force 1925-1955." In *The Condominium Remembered : The Making of the Sudanese State*, edited by Levin, Deborah, 99-100. Vol. 1. Durham : University of Durham Press, 1991.

"F.R.H. Own's Reaction to 1946 Southern Policy, January 5, 1946" In Beshir's *Southern Sudan" Background to Conflict*, pp. 127-29.

"President of SANU, Mr. William Deng on the Coming Elections" *SANU Youth Monthly Bulletin*, 2 (November 1967), p. 1.

"Proceedings of the Juba Conference on the Political Development of the Southern Sudan, Juba, June 12-13, 1947" In Beshir's *The Southern Sudan: Background to Conflict, pp. 136-53.*

Riak, Aliar, "The Public Reactions on the Assassination of the SANU President, William Deng" *SANU Youth Organ Monthly Bulletin* 8 (July 1968), pp. 16-19.

Richova, Praha Blanka, "The Ethnic Conflict as the Factor of State coherence in Africa: The Case of the Sudan" *Archive Orientalni* 59 (1991), pp. 289-312.

Robertshow, Peter. 1987. "Prehistory in Upper Nile Basin". *Journal of African History* 28 (2):177-189

Robertson, James. "The Sudan in Transition." *African Affairs* 52 (1953): 317-27.

Robinson, D. "AnyaNya Revolt." *Newsweek* 74 (13 October 1969) : 60+.

Russell, Peter and Storrs MacCall, "Can Succession be Justified? The Case of the Southern Sudan" In *The Southern Sudan and the Problem of National Integration*, pp. 93-119.

"SANU Appeals to Mahjoub's Government to Rectify the Choatic Situation in the South" *SANU Youth Organ Monthly Bulletin* 8 (1968), pp. 5-8.

Sarkensian, Sam C. "The Southern Sudan: A Reassessment" *African Studies Review* 16 (1973), pp. 1-22.

Sconyers, David Joseph. "Hurrying Home: Sudanization and National Integration, 1953-1956." *British Society for Middle Eastern Studies Bulletin* 15, no. 192 (1988) : 64-94.

Shaffer, N. Manfred, "The Sudan: Arab-African Confrontation" *Current History* (1966), pp. 142-47.

Sharma, B. S., "The 1965 Elections in the Sudan" *The Political Quarterly* 37, 4 (1966), pp. 441-52.

Sid Ahmed, S.M., "Christian Missionary Activities in Sudan 1926-1948" in *Southern Sudan: Religionalism and Religion,* edited by Mohammed O. Beshir (Khartoum: University of Khartoum press, 1984), pp. 241-76.

Stevens, Richard P., "The 1972 Addis Ababa Agreement and the Sudan's Afro-Arab Policy" *The Journal of Modern African Studies,* 14, 2 (1976), pp. 247-274.

Teraifi, Al-Ayoub Al-. "Sudanization of the Public Service: Critical Analysis." *Sudan Notes and Records* LVIII (1977) : 117-134.

Ushari, Ahmed Mahmud. "Arabic in the Southern Sudan: History and Spread of Pidgin Creole." *International Journal of Sociology of Language* 61 (1986): 113-116.

Wakoson, Elias Nyamlell. "The Origin and Development of the AnyaNya Movement 1955-1972" In *Southern Sudan; Regionalisms and Religion,* edited by Mohammed O. Beshir (University of Khartoum 1984), pp. 127-204.

Warburg, Gabriel R. "National Identity in the Sudan: Fact, Fiction and Prejudice in Ethnic and Religious Relations." *Asian and African Studies* 24 (1990) : 151-202.

Wassara, Samson S. and Abdel Magid A. Bob, "The Emergence of Organized Political Movement in Southern Sudan 1946-1972" In *The Nationalist Movement in the Sudan,* edited by Mahasin Abdel Gadir Haj a-Safi,(Khartoum: University of Khartoum, 1989), pp. 295-321.

Woodward, Peter, "The South in Sudanese Politics, 1946-1956" *Middle Eastern Studies,* 16, No, 3 (1980), pp. 178-92.

_____, "Nationalism and Opposition in the Sudan" *African Affairs* 80 (1981), pp. 379-388.

Yoh, John G. Nyuot. "Waqia al-harb bayn junub wa-shamal al-Sudan" *As-Safir* (Beirut), Part I, 12 December 1992, issue no. 6359; Part II, 14 December 1992, issue no. 6360. (In Arabic)

_____, "Southern Sudan: A Quest for Identity?." *Zavarian Review* (Beirut) XVI, (2 December 1993), pp. 10-11.

_____, "Hal yushakkil infisal junub al-sudan tahdidan fi'aliyyan li-Misr?." *Al-Hayat* (London) 8 April 1994, issue no. 11374. (In Arabic)

_____, "Al-Qiwa al-siyasiyya al-sudaniyya wa-shurutihem li-salam fi al-junub." *An-Nahar* (Beirut) 23 July 1994, issue no. 18888. (In Arabic)

_____, "Maktabat al-harb al-Sudaniyya." *Al-Hayat* (London) 5 August 1994, issue no. 11492. (In Arabic)

_____, "The Sudan Defense Corps: A Historical Overview, 1924-1955." *Lebanese National Defense* (Beirut), April 1995, issue No. 12.

_____, "Al-Hiwar bayn al-Masihiyyun wal-Muslimun fi al-Sudan: Ila ayn?." *Al-Nashra* (Amman) 16 September 1996. Vol. 1. (In Arabic)

_____, "al-Masihiyyun fi al-Sudan al-yuo'm." *Al-Nashra*, (Amman) 16 September 1997. Vol. 5.

_____,"Al-Muthaqqaf al-Sudani wal-Khyarat al-sa'ba." *An Nahar* (Beirut), 8 January 1998. (In Arabic)

_____, "The Dynamics of War and Peace in Sudan." *Conflict Trends* (Durban) No. 4 (2001): 28-37.

3. Theses and Dissertations

Abdun, Farouk Akasha, "Education and Integration in the Sudan: A Historical Review" (Unpublished M. A. Thesis: Beirut, American University of Beirut, 1987), pp. 16-26.

Abu Agla, Sidig Y. "The Regional Autonomy in the Southern Sudan." M.A. Thesis, American University of Beirut, 1977.

Akuay, Deng Dongrin. "Political Consequences of Uneven Development in Sudan: An Analysis of Political Struggles with Special Reference to SPLM/SPLA." PhD. diss., University of Hull, 1990.

Badal, Raphael K. "British Administration in Southern Sudan." PhD. diss., University of London, 1970.

Bakheit, J. M. "Britain Administration and Sudanese Nationalism, 1919-1939." PhD diss., University of Cambridge, 1965.

Blowei, Philip Chol. "Educational Development in Southern Sudan during the British Administration." M.Sc. Thesis, University of Khartoum, 1978.

Cudsi, A. S. "Sudanese Resistance to British Rule, 1900-1920." M.Sc. Thesis, University of Khartoum, 1969.

_____. "The Rise of Political Parties in Northern Sudan, 1936-46." PhD diss., University of London, 1978.

Digernes, O. "Appearance and Reality in Southern Sudan: A Study of the British Administration of the Nuer, 1900-30." Thesis for the degree of Cand. Polit., University of Bergen, Norway, 1978.

Duany, Michael Wal. "Neither Palaces nor Prisons: The Constitution of Order among the Nuer." PhD diss., Indiana University, 1992.

El-Bashir, Ahmed E. "Confrontation Across the Sudd: Southern Sudan's Struggle for Freedom, 1839-1955." PhD dissertation, Howard University, Washington DC, 1979.

Fifer, William A. "Sudanese Independence and Its Problems." M.Sc. Thesis, American University of Beirut, 1962.

Grandin-Blanc, N. "Le Soudan nilotique et son administration coloniale britannique." Thése pour le Doctorat de 3éme Cycle, Paris, 1975.

Hanes, William Traves. "The Rise and Fall of the Sudan Political Service: A British View of Decolonization in Anglo-Egyptian Sudan." PhD diss., University of Texas, Austin, 1990.

Howell, John. "Political Leadership and Organization in Southern Sudan." PhD dissertation, University of Reading, Reading, 1978, p. 265.

Jal, Gabriel Giet. "The Question of the Sudan in Anglo-Egyptian Treaty of 1936." M.A. Thesis, American University of Beirut, 1978.

_____. "The History of the Jikany Nuer Before 1920." PhD diss., University of London, 1987.

Johnson, Douglas H. "History and Prophesy Among the Nuer of Southern Sudan." PhD diss., University of California, 1980.

Loiria, Angelo Lobale. « Political Awakening in Southern Sudan, 1946-1955 : Decolonialization and the Problem of National Integration. » PhD diss., University of California, 1969.

Madut, Andrew Malek. « The Effects of Culture on Mnagaement Practices in the Public Service Organizations in the Southern Sudan. » PhD diss., University of Glasgow, 1986.

Mahamoud, Abd Al-Rahim A. « Development of Administration and Public Policies in the Sudan, 1970-1982. » PhD diss., University of Reading, 1984.

Majak, Damasio Dutt. "British Rule in Bahr el Ghazal, 1907-1927." MA Thesis, University of Khartoum, 1976.

Mulla, Richard Kabi. "Decentralization in the Sudan." PhD diss., University of London, 1986.

Mustafa, Umar Abdin. "Emin Pasha in the Equatorial Province: A Study of Challenges and Achievements." M.A. Thesis, American University of Beirut, 1971.

Pitya, Philip Legge. "History of Western Christian Evangelism in Sudan, 1898-1964." PhD diss, Boston University, 1996.

lo Polito, Nicola. "The Verona Fathers in Southern Sudan from 1899 to 1964." MA Thesis, Catholic Theological Union, Chicago, 1986.

Salih, Mohammed Ali, "The Round Table Conference and the Search for a Constitutional Solution to the Problem of the Southern Sudan" M. Sc. University of Khartoum, 1971.

Salim, Galobouri Mohamed. "Pattern of Decentralization in the Republic of the Sudan." M.A. Thesis, New York University, 1962.

Sanderson, Lilian M. "Education in the Southern Sudan, 1899-1948." PhD diss., University of London, 1966.

Sconyers, David Joseph. "British Policy and Mission Education in the Southern Sudan, 1928-1946." PhD diss., University of Pennsylvania, 1978.

Sevier, C. E. "The Anglo-Egyptian Condominium in the Southern Sudan, 1918-1939." PhD diss., Princeton University, 1975.

Wawa, Yosa H. "Southern Sudan: History and Trends in Research." M.A. thesis, Longborough University, 1994.

Wol, Lawrence Wol. "Réflexions sur la conscience nationale au sud-Soudan." These de 3éme Cycle, Bordeaux, 1971.

Woodward, Peter R. "The Condominium and Sudanese Nationalism, 1942-1955." PhD diss., University of Reading, 1975.

Yoh, John G. "The Torit Mutiny, August 1955" MA thesis, American University of Beirut, February 1995.

4. Reports and research papers

Ajawain, Yoanes Yor Akol. *Administration of Justice and Legal Aid*. A paper presented to the Steering Committee for Human Rights in the Transition in Sudan. Kampala, Uganda, 8-12 February 1999.

_____, *Human Rights Violations and Transitional Justice*. A paper presented to the Steering Committee for Human Rights in the Transition in Sudan. Kampala, Uganda, 8-12 February 1999.

Constitution of the Republic of Sudan. Khartoum, 1 July 1998.

de Chand, David. *The Right of Self-Determination: A Legal and Political Right for the South Sudan*. Unpublished manuscript. Nairobi, August 1995.

Duany, Wal and Julia Aker Dunay. *Grasping for a Democratic Peace in the Sudan*. Workshop in Political Theory and Policy Analysis, Indiana: Indiana University, May 1999.

Eprile, Cecil L. *Sudan: The Long War*. London: Institute for the Study of Conflict, 1972.

Evans-Pritchard, Sir Edward E. *Administrative Problems in Southern Sudan*. Oxford: Clarendon Press, 1938.

Field, Shannon. *The Civil War in Sudan: The Role of the Oil Industry*. (IGD Occasional Paper No. 23). The Institute for Global Dialogue. Braamfontein, South Africa, February 2000.

God, Oil, and Country: Changing the Logic of War in Sudan. ICS Africa Report No. 39. Brussels: International Crisis Group, 2002.

Khartoum (Sudan) Peace Agreement. Khartoum, 21 April 1997.

Lagu, Joseph. *Chronology of the North-South Conflict in the Sudan*. Unpublished manuscript. London, 2000. 15 pages.

Lueth, John Akech. *Political Development in the Southern Sudan Armed Movement*. Juba : University of Juba, 1980.

Jok, John Luk. *The Right of Self-Determination in Southern Sudan : Mechanisms for Implementation*. A paper presented to the Steering Committee for Human Rights in the Transition in Sudan. Kampala, Uganda, 8-12 February 1999.

_____, *Constitutional Options for Southern Sudan*. A paper presented to the Steering Committee for Human Rights in the Transition in Sudan. Kampala, Uganda, 8-12 February 1999.

Morrison, G. *The Southern Sudan and Eritrea: Aspects of a Wider African Problem*. London: Minority Rights Group, Report No. 5, 1973.

Peace and Unity in the Sudan: An African Achievement. Khartoum: Ministry of Foreign Affairs, 1975.

Rahal, Musa Suleiman. *The Marginalised Areas of the Northern Sudan and the Question of Self-Determination*. A paper presented to the Steering Committee for Human Rights in the Transition in Sudan. Kampala, Uganda, 8-12 February 1999.

Teny-Dhurgon, Riek Machar. *South Sudan: A History of Political Domination, a Case for Self-Determination*. Unpublished manuscript. Nairobi, November 1995.

Verona Fathers' Mission. *Sudan Government Secret Plans Against Christian Missions in the South*, n.p., n.d. (?1965)..

Wakoson, Elias Nyamlell. *Southern Sudan: The Political Leadership of the AnyaNya Movement*. Juba: University of Juba, 1980.

Wanji, Barri-Naggara. *The National and Nationality Questions and the Rise of the African Sate of South Sudan: A Model.* A Paradigm to be presented to the Steering Committee of South Sudan Civic Forum, scheduled to be held on 12-17 November 2001, Abuja, Nigeria.

_____, The Holocaust: Sudan's Afro-Arab War of Slavery and Genocide, 1821-2002. Nairobi, Kenya. Manuscript of a forthcoming book. Ethnic Communities in South Sudan

JOHN GAI YOH holds BA in Political Science and MA in political history from the American University of Beirut (AUB) and PhD in International Politics from University of South Africa in Pretoria. His assignments included Presidential Advisor on Education, Minister of Education, Science & Technology, Head of Government of Southern Sudan (GOSS) Southern African Liaison Office, Pretoria. He also served as South Sudan Ambassador to the Republic of Turkey. Was Resident Research Associate at the Royal Institute for Inter-Faith Studies, Amman, Jordan between July 1996 and May 2003 as well as lecturer at University of South Africa in Pretoria between June 2003-June 2007. He authored several works on Africa, East Africa, Sudan, international politics, conflict management and resolution, regional and international organizations, security and strategic studies.